DESIGNER GENES

TALKING POINT

DESIGNER GENES

Phil Gates

Cover illustration by
Mark Thomas

SCHOLASTIC

Scholastic Children's Books,
Commonwealth House, 1-19 New Oxford Street
London WC1A 1NU, UK
A division of Scholastic Ltd
London ~ New York ~ Toronto ~ Sydney ~ Auckland

Published in the UK by Scholastic Ltd, 1998

ISBN 0 590 19017 2

Printed by Cox & Wyman Ltd, Reading, Berks
Typeset by Rapid Reprographics Ltd

10 9 8 7 6 5 4 3 2 1

CONTENTS

About this book

Some people say that modern science could turn us into cannibals.

They don't mean that we'll soon be tucking into lumps of people instead of chunks of cows for Sunday lunch. It's subtler than that.

Scientists have learned how to move genes between living organisms in ways that can never occur in nature. They can put human genes in farm animals, for example, to make them grow faster, larger and leaner. So if you ate a steak or a chop from one of these animals, you'd be eating products of your own genes. It's not the familiar kind of horror-movie cannibalism, maybe, but it's still something that would have been unthinkable just a few years ago.

Genes are Nature's master plans for all living things. Scientists' understanding of the way they work has advanced by leaps and bounds over the last ten years. By looking at the genes that fate dealt you at birth, some researchers claim they will soon be able to tell whether you'll be intelligent, mentally ill, violent, or even homosexual. They can already find out whether you carry inherited diseases that will strike you down in the future.

This is dangerous information, in the wrong hands. It could stop you getting a job, for example. Information based on people's genes has already sent thousands of criminals – and some innocent people – to prison.

Information about your genes can be psychologically devastating. If you discover you've got dud genes, should you risk having children and passing the same defect to them? And do you really want to live with the knowledge that you carry genes for a life-threatening genetic disease that will destroy your brain before you reach 50? Geneticists can confront us with new information like this and present us with choices that most of us never expected to have to make. There are quite a few people who are not sure whether they really want to know so much about themselves.

The new technology that lets scientists redraw nature's plans by shuffling genes between almost any living organisms is called genetic engineering. Some scientists are confident that they can use this technology to improve plants, animals or even people, in much the same way that you might upgrade a computer by fitting it with a faster microchip. But who is to say exactly what an 'improvement' might be? Who should decide whether we really want plants that can make plastics, farm animals that make drugs in their milk and people whose length of life can be doubled?

Even some scientists say that decisions like this shouldn't be left to them. They are decisions that should involve everyone. After all, they'll touch all our lives, in one way or another.

You may have already eaten genetically engineered food without realizing it. Currently, there's no law in Britain to force the food industry to label all products that have been treated in this way. Scientists are developing genetic engineering technology faster than most people realize. If you want to have a say in how it should be used, you need to know how it works and what it can do.

And that's what this book is about.

'I believe we have now reached a moral and ethical watershed. What actual right do we have to experiment, Frankenstein-like, with the very stuff of life?'
(HRH Prince Charles, in a speech to organic farmers, 1996)

Section One
WOULD YOU RATHER BE A PIG?

The phone rings. It's bad news. A member of your family has had a heart attack. You rush to their hospital bedside.

The doctor takes you to one side and tells you that the patient's heart is so badly damaged that there's only one way to save them – with a heart transplant. If they don't get one, they'll die. The hospital can carry out the operation, but there's a problem – there are no donor hearts available.

'But don't worry,' she says, 'we can use a pig's heart instead.' She goes on to explain that genetic engineering technology has produced pigs with hearts that can be transplanted into humans.

Science fiction? Not at all. Pig hearts are already available that could be transplanted into humans. The companies that own them are just waiting for permission to try it out. And demand is so great that it's only a matter of time before they go ahead.

Heart swap history

➤The first attempt to transplant a human heart was made by Dr Christiaan Barnard in South Africa in 1967. Then, the patient died quickly, but today the same operation can extend a life by twenty years. All kinds of human organ transplants save thousands of lives every year. They're becoming more successful all the time, mainly because new drugs like cyclosporin are used to disarm the natural defence system of the human body and prevent it from rejecting transplanted organs.

Transplants save lives and money. A kidney transplant costs £10,000, and the patient needs £3000 worth of drugs every year to keep them alive. It currently costs £18,000 every year to treat the same patient if a dialysis machine is used to do the work of their kidney and remove lethal waste products from their blood.

So it's hardly surprising that demand for organ transplants has risen, and that there just aren't enough spare organs to go round. Now, in the US alone, around 100,000 human organs are needed every year for transplant patients. In Britain, over 300 desperately ill patients are waiting for a new heart.

The problem is that too few young people with healthy hearts, kidneys and livers are killed in road accidents. They're the best source of human spare parts, and there would have to be absolute carnage on our roads before enough spare organs were available to meet spare-part demand.

Many people like the idea of donating organs to keep someone else alive, but only 25 per cent of the British population carry an organ donor card. Some countries, like Belgium and Singapore, have tried to satisfy demand for spare parts by assuming that all people will be donors. There, doctors will automatically use your organs after you die, unless you register your refusal during your lifetime.

So, to find enough vital organs, doctors have to look elsewhere. Mechanical hearts have been tried, but it will be many years before they're perfected. The only other option is to use organs from other animals.

Xenotransplantation – the triumphs and the tragedies

Xenotransplantation is the scientific term for transplanting animal organs into people. This is the story so far:

1964 – Six people receive chimp kidneys – one survives for nine months. The rest die in a few days. In the same year six patients supplied with baboon kidneys die within two months. The first pig heart valve transplant takes place – this is now a routine operation in hospitals.

1968 – Patient dies instantly after receiving a sheep's heart.

1984 – Baby with a transplanted baboon's heart dies in 20 days.

1992 – Patient with a pig's heart dies in less than 24 hours.

1992 – Patient survives for 70 days with a baboon liver.

1994– Ten Swedish diabetics, whose pancreases can't control their blood sugar levels, receive pig pancreas cells. The pig cells work for 14 months in four patients.

1995 – Jeff Getty, an AIDS patient in the USA, receives baboon bone marrow transplant, to produce large quantities of HIV resistant white blood cells.

1997 – Fears grow that transplanting animal organs into people could spread deadly animal diseases into people. A British Government Committee recommends banning these transplants until all risks are properly understood.

1997 – In India a surgeon is arrested after illegally transplanting a pig's heart into his patient. The patient dies.

Monkey business

➤Which animals could supply us with spare parts?

Monkeys and chimpanzees might help. Chimpanzees are our closest relatives. Chimps and humans evolved from a common ancestor just a few million years ago and this means that we share 98.4 per cent of our genes with them. This basic similarity means that chimp-human transplants are more likely to succeed than those with any other donor species.

Genespeak
Ethics – the science used to decide whether human activities are morally right or wrong.

To decide whether an action is morally right, you need to consider whether it (a) restricts freedom; (b) causes injustice; (c) causes harm; (d) is unkind. If you can answer 'yes' to any of these, then the action may not be moral.

But in many ways they are too much like us. They smile. They play. They feel pain just like us – and show it. And they're cute and cuddly. Is it ethically right to kill animals that feel pain and emotion, just so that we can steal their body parts?

There's a practical problem too. Chimps are an endangered species. If we were to kill 10,000 chimps a year for spare parts, they'd soon be extinct. They don't breed fast enough in captivity to meet the demand for transplant organs either, so that's not an option.

Disease danger

➤And then there's the fear of infection. Monkeys carry diseases that we can catch. Macaque monkeys, which have been used in transplant experiments, carry a form of herpes B virus that can cause a fatal brain infection in humans.

We might transplant such viruses from monkey bodies into our own. Remember, when organs are transplanted into people, the patient's immune system has to be disarmed with cyclosporin, so they don't reject the transplanted organ. This means that they also catch infections and diseases very easily.

Deadly viruses have jumped from monkeys to humans before. In 1967 workers in a factory at Marburg in Germany began to suffer from a mystery disease. The factory used monkeys, imported from Africa, to make vaccines. One by one, the workers collapsed with headaches and raging fevers, then began to bleed uncontrollably from their noses, eyes, mouths and all the other orifices of their bodies. A quarter of them died, victims of what came to be known as Marburg virus, carried by the monkeys. Since then an even more deadly virus – Ebola – has probably been passed from monkeys to people. When that strikes, it can kill nine out of ten of its victims.

So you can easily imagine what might happen if a patient fitted with a monkey heart caught a new disease, that they could pass on to other people. They might start an epidemic that would be far worse than AIDS.

Enter the pig

➤So monkey heart transplants are fraught with dangers. Most scientists now agree that pig spare parts are a better bet.

There are fewer problems with pigs, unless you're a vegetarian. We eat pork already. How can you object to a heart transplant from a pig if you enjoy a bacon sandwich for breakfast? And pigs breed fast, as well as having large litters, so they'll never be in short supply.

We are less likely to catch diseases from them too, because they're not closely related to us, although we would still need to be extremely careful.

'What animal [pig] organ recipients should really be advised of, if they want to steer clear of infection, is to reconsider any plans that they might have for a career in pig-farming.' (Editorial, NatureBiotechnology, 1996)

Pig hearts are very similar to human hearts, but until now it's proved impossible to transplant them into our bodies. The human immune system, which fights diseases by attacking any foreign cells that it detects, automatically rejects transplanted organs from other animals. But in 1995 genetic engineers successfully altered pig immune system genes to match our own. Now our bodies can be fooled into accepting pig spare parts.

So xenotransplants from pigs are almost here. By the end of 1996 a company that breeds genetically engineered transplant pigs announced that it was nearly ready to supply spare part hearts, if it was allowed to. Then last-minute doubts set in.

A British government committee warned that the

transplants should be banned until the risks were better understood. That may have been a wise move. In 1997 some scientists who re-examined preserved lungs from people who had died of an influenza epidemic in 1918 discovered that the virus that killed them probably came from pigs. That, flu epidemic killed 600,000 people in the USA, and maybe as many as 50 million worldwide. It was probably started by someone just being in contact with an infected pig. If that could cause such a terrible disaster, what horrors might be unleashed if virus-infected pig organs were transplanted into people's bodies? It's a chilling thought, and one that makes medical scientists proceed with great caution.

But, once the genetically-engineered pigs receive a clean bill of health, it seems certain that pig-to-people heart transplants will soon become a routine operation. Desperately ill patients are already waiting.

Last minute questions

➤'Any questions you'd like to ask me?' says the doctor, as they wheel your loved one away for surgery and prepare to kill a suitable pig.

Plenty, probably.

How can you be sure that the operation will work? Can you be sure that the genetic engineers who made the transplant possible really knew what they were doing? You need reassurance. You need to know why doctors are so confident. You need a crash course in genetic engineering.

It's a tale of peas, parasites, pus, fruit flies, bacteria and a pair of Cambridge scientists with a passion for making models.

Section Two
GENETIC ENGINEERING A CRASH COURSE FOR THE CURIOUS

The rules of life are not written in words, but in genes. Genes are chemical codes inside your cells that control your appearance, your survival and even perhaps the way you behave. It's taken scientists 150 years to find them and unlock their secrets.

The germination of an idea

➤Gregor Mendel started it all. He was a peasant's son who eventually became Abbot of the monastery at Brünn, in the country we now call the Czech Republic. In the 1860s he became fascinated by a question that had perplexed the world's great thinkers since the beginning of recorded history: how are characteristics that we inherit passed on from parents to children?

Mendel, like all great scientists, was motivated by curiosity. He tested his theories by carrying out experiments, not with people, but with peas. He carefully cultivated rows of plants that were selected for different features. Some were tall, others were short. There were plants with white flowers and coloured flowers, green pods and yellow pods. Some rows produced seeds of different shapes. In his experiments he carefully transferred pollen between the different types of peas, crossing and recrossing plants to produce seeds from different combinations of parents.

Mendel was a mathematician, and when he analysed his results a pattern began to emerge in his columns of figures. He soon noticed that his plants seemed to be obeying fixed laws that determined how characteristics were passed on from parents to offspring.

These laws, which later became known as Mendel's Laws of Inheritance, allowed him to predict what the offspring of his plants would look like just by looking at the characteristics of the parents. If you had asked him which plants you needed to cross to produce dwarf pea plants with wrinkled seeds, white flowers and yellow pods, he could have told you in an instant.

Mendel could make these seemingly magical predictions because he understood that the characteristics of living things were controlled by invisible particles that were passed on from parents to offspring. Once you understood the rules that controlled the way that the particles from parents combined, you could easily predict what their offspring would look like.

Doctors today use the same laws to predict whether children born to certain parents may suffer from certain conditions and diseases. Scientists who breed new crops still use the same laws to help them decide which plants they should cross-pollinate in order to produce better crops.

Mendel published his discoveries in 1866, but no one realized how important they were until 1900, when his 'particles' were given a name – genes. It comes from a Greek word – genos – which means descent. Genes are the particles that are passed on from ancestors to their descendants.

The science of genes – genetics – had begun.

The dance of the chromosomes

➤The invention of microscopes in the early 17th century revealed that all living organisms are made up of minute, individual cells, but it wasn't until the end of the 19th century that microscope lenses were powerful enough for scientists to explore the inner workings of a cell. Then, in the 1880s, scientists who were examining worms that lived in horses' intestines began to report sightings of strange, thread-like objects that seemed to float in the watery contents of the worm's cells.

When the cells were about to divide, the threads went through a series of elegant, complicated movements, like dancers in a ballet. The threads paired up, divided, then separated into new cells, so that copies of each thread were distributed to each daughter cell. The cycle was repeated over and over again, every time a cell divided.

Genespeak
Chromosomes – thread-like structures in cells, made up of long strings of thousands of genes.

When Mendel's Laws were rediscovered in 1900 scientists began to look for genes inside cells. It turned out that they were located on these dancing threads, that became known as chromosomes.

The man who found them was Thomas Hunt Morgan, a professor at Columbia University in New York.

Morgan's maps

➤Morgan was permanently surrounded by fruit flies. If you'd visited his laboratory, you'd have noticed a faint smell of over-ripe fruit and would have been constantly irritated by tiny insects that escaped from captivity. He carried out his genetic experiments on fruit flies because they breed fast, in enormous numbers. You could do a lot of experiments quickly, raising flies in bottles and feeding them on stewed bananas and oatmeal. Morgan could get answers to big questions in just a couple of weeks.

By the end of the First World War Morgan and his

colleagues had proved that genes were strung out in sequence along chromosomes. As his research team delved deeper into the workings of chromosomes they discovered that the position of the genes, which controlled every characteristic of the flies, could be mapped along the chromosome, like cities, towns and villages spaced out along a highway.

So now scientists knew how genes were inherited. They knew where they were. But what were they made of?

The magic molecule

➤The first clue could already be found in the research of a German biochemist called Johann Friedrich Miescher, who was a regular visitor to hospital wards where patients suffered from septic wounds.

Genespeak
White blood cells – colourless cells in the blood system, whose job is to fight infections.
Nucleus – the control centre of the cell, where chromosomes and genes are located.

Miescher wanted to isolate the chemical components of blood cells, but he found it difficult to get enough suitable cells to work on. The bandages removed from hospital patients provided the perfect opportunity. The pus that oozed from septic wounds was full of white blood cells, which the patient's body produced to fight infections.

Armed with a collection of pus-soaked bandages, Miescher retreated to his laboratory and began to isolate the chemical compounds from the cells. By 1870 he had found one particularly interesting group of chemicals in the central nucleus of cells. Later, it was discovered that the nucleus also happened to be the place where you could find chromosomes when the cells weren't dividing.

Miescher called the compounds that he found there 'nucleic acids'. Much later, in 1944, an American doctor called Oswald Theodore Avery proved that nucleic acids were indeed the molecules that genes were made of.

Genespeak
Bacteria – microscopic, single-celled organisms that are found everywhere. Some are useful, others cause diseases.

Avery became fascinated by the sexual habits of bacteria. In 1944 he discovered that bacteria had sex, and passed on genes to one another, by transferring nucleic acids from cell to cell. The nucleic acids behaved just like Mendel's famous particles. Unfortunately no one took much notice of Avery's pioneering work until the early 1950s.

Doodling DNA

Genespeak
DNA – the chemical molecule that genes are made from.

➤Then James Watson, Francis Crick and Rosalind Franklin, a trio of scientists at Cambridge University, used X-rays to explore the structure of one particular kind of nucleic acid molecule, called deoxyribonucleic acid – better known as DNA. Rosalind Franklin worked away in the laboratory, firing X-rays at DNA crystals and recording the way that the rays ricocheted around the lab. Watson and Crick retreated to the local pub, trying to work out what her results meant.

After many hours of drinking and doodling on scraps of paper they returned to the lab and built a model of the molecule. DNA turned out to have a strange, helical shape that looked like a spiral staircase.

DNA turned out to be the stuff that the genes on the chromosomes were made of. The discovery eventually earned Watson and Crick a Nobel Prize in 1962. Franklin was unlucky. Tragically, she died from cancer in 1958 and never enjoyed the fame and international honours heaped on her two male colleagues.

So now scientists knew how genes were passed on. They knew where to find them. They'd found out what they were made of. But how did they work?

One small step on life's spiral staircase

➤Watson and Crick solved this problem too.

DNA is a spiral staircase-shaped molecule. The sides of the 'spiral staircase' are held together by four different kinds of chemical unit, called bases. The bases are joined in pairs and arranged like the steps of the staircase.

It soon became obvious how DNA molecules divided. The 'steps' made from bases separated from one another so that the whole 'spiral staircase' split down the middle. It was like a zip being undone, separating the DNA molecule lengthwise into two halves. Then each of the halves rebuilt a matching half from spare molecules floating around inside the cell. In this way the original DNA molecule made exact copies of itself, which were then shared between cells when they divided.

Mendel's magic particles were molecules of DNA, that passed information on from one generation to the next. But how could a DNA molecule possibly contain all the information needed to build living organisms?

Watson and Crick thought they knew the answer. It must be some kind of code.

Codebreaking

Genespeak
Protein – chemical compounds that are essential parts of the structure of all living cells.
Amino acid – the small chemical units that proteins are built from.
Enzymes – molecules that dismantle or reassemble other molecules.

➤Cells that make bodies are mainly constructed from chemicals called proteins, and not from DNA. The proteins themselves are constructed from many different kinds of building blocks, called amino acids. What was the relationship between DNA, amino acids and genes?

Watson and Crick discovered that the bases that formed the 'steps' of the spiral staircase-shaped DNA molecule acted as a chemical code.

The bases were grouped in threes. Each group of three bases (or 'steps' in the 'spiral staircase') was a code for a different amino acid. The cell could read the code, working from one end of the DNA molecule to the other. As the code was read, the amino acids were lined up, spliced together and made into proteins which were released into the cells to do their work. The DNA molecule was the blueprint for proteins, that were used to build cells.

DNA - A living Lego kit

➤Driven by curiosity, scientists began to wonder whether it might be possible to change the genetic code, and maybe modify life itself. What would happen if you cut out pieces of the genetic code and moved them between living organisms?

The opportunity to find out came in 1968, when a Swiss scientist called Werner Arber discovered enzymes that could chop DNA into pieces that could then be rejoined in different ways.

Scientists soon learned to use the enzymes to cut pieces of DNA from plant and animal cells and splice them into DNA inside bacteria, so the bacteria would make proteins that would normally only be made by the plants and animals. The process, which was a bit like building a new, living machine from spare parts, became known as genetic engineering. Bits of DNA could be used like living Lego bricks to build new organisms.

At first it was not much more than an interesting laboratory experiment, which could tell scientists more about how genes worked. But soon it became obvious that some genes could be used to redesign organisms in ways that might be useful.

Some business-minded technologists – who soon became known as biotechnologists – realized that they could use this technology to design products that had the potential to generate huge commercial profits. And so the genetic engineering industry was born, and the day of the designer organism, fitted with designer genes to the customer's specification, had arrived.

Within twenty years of Arber's discovery, genetic engineers were swapping genes around all over the place.

Genes from bacteria that killed pests were put into crop plants, so pests that fed on the crops would die. Scorpion genes were put into viruses that infected caterpillars, to make the viruses more efficient killers of these insect pests.

And human genes found their way into pigs. One of them was a gene that controls the human immune response. It prevents our bodies from recognizing and trying to attack organs taken from pigs that are transplanted into us.

And that's the gene that allows pig hearts to be transplanted into people.

'With genetic engineering and gene-splicing we can stitch, edit, recombine and programme living materials across biological boundaries, creating novel forms of life. Nature has clearly prescribed limits with what we can do. With genetic technology these limits become irrelevant.'
(Jeremy Rifkin, American Environmentalist)

Section Three
BEATING THE LOTTERY OF LIFE
8
39
19
31
42
16
10
39
12

You have 46 chromosomes, in 23 matched pairs, in every cell of your body – except for the sex cells in your ovaries or testes, which only carry one of each pair of chromosomes.

Genespeak
Mutant – an organism that carries a mutation.
Mutation – a spontaneous change in a gene, which may produce a difference in its owner.

If you carry a mutated gene on a single chromosome it won't affect you, because your body also contains an unchanged copy of the gene on the matching sister chromosome. In this case, the mutant copy of the gene is said to be recessive to the normal (dominant) copy on the sister chromosome. The effect of the normal gene smothers any damaging effect of a single mutant copy. A geneticist would describe you as being heterozygous for the mutant gene.

Mutant genes only have a visible effect if they occur in both copies of a matched pair of chromosomes. If a person carries a copy of a mutant gene on both chromosomes of a pair in this way, then geneticists describe them as being homozygous.

Imagine the situation where a mother and father both carry a mutant gene in a heterozygous condition, so neither parent shows any visible symptoms of the mutation. When the mother produces egg cells, and the father produces sperm, each of these reproductive cells only contains 23 chromosomes – one from each matched pair. So half the egg cells will contain a mutant version of the gene, and half will carry the unaltered version. The same is true of the sperm cells – only half of them will carry the mutation.

When a mutant sperm cell meets a mutant egg cell, an embryo is formed with 46 chromosomes (23 matched pairs) again. But now one of those pairs of chromosomes will carry a pair of mutant genes. The mutation is now in the homozygous state, and that means it can have an effect.

Inheritance is life's lottery and the mutant genes that we pass on to our children have always been a matter of good or bad luck – until geneticists got to work.

Passing on mutations

➤Suppose that you have a gene called X on one of your chromosomes and a mutant version of the gene, x, on the matching chromosome of the pair. You'll produce two kinds of sex cells, that can either contain the X gene or the mutant gene, but not both.

Now imagine that you meet a partner with exactly the same mutation on one of their chromosomes and decide to have a child. When your sex cells join up to form an embryo, it could inherit four different combinations of X and x genes, like this:

Father's sperm cells

Mother's egg cells	**X**	**x**
X	**XX** NORMAL	**Xx** NORMAL
x	**Xx** NORMAL	**xx**

Only children with this mutant gene combination shows its effects

If your child has the XX gene combination, it will be fine.

If it carries the Xx combination, it won't have any

problems, because the dominant X gene on one chromosome will swamp the effect of the mutant x gene on a sister chromosome.

But there's a one-in-four chance that your child will be born with a pair of mutant genes, xx, and show the effect of the mutation.

Gregor Mendel worked this out nearly 140 years ago. This is the way in which we inherit most of our characteristics, ranging from harmless variations like hair colour and eye colour to inconvenient and even dangerous genetic defects like colour blindness, although the pattern of inheritance is much more complicated when many genes are involved, rather than the single one that's shown in this example.

Pay your money, make your choice

➤Today, for a modest fee, you can spit into a test tube, post it to a genetic testing company and find out whether you carry a mutant gene for a genetic disorder called cystic fibrosis. Scientists in their laboratory can examine the DNA in cells in your saliva and tell whether it carries mutant genes that your future children might inherit.

Why should you want to know? Well, consider the case of Michael, a five-year-old who is one of 300 children born with cystic fibrosis in Britain every year.

'Michael seemed perfectly healthy when he was born,' says his mother, 'so it was a terrible shock when we took him for a check-up with what seemed like a bad cough, and the doctor discovered that our son had cystic fibrosis.'

'Neither of us has the disease, but what we didn't know was that we both carry a single copy of a defective gene. Michael inherited it from both of us, and with two copies he's developed the disease,' explained his father.

Cystic fibrosis makes the linings of Michael's lungs dry out, so they become coated in thick mucous. He has difficulty breathing sometimes and he constantly runs the risk of serious lung infections.

'Every night we have to lay him face down and hit his back, to loosen the mucous. It's distressing for him and for us.'

But what's most distressing for Michael's parents is the knowledge that their son's chances of survival beyond his late twenties are slim, unless science comes up with a cure before the disease kills him.

Cystic fibrosis, the commonest inherited disease, is most often caused by a defective gene known as CFTR, so some couples prefer to find out whether they carry the gene before they decide to have children. All they need is a sample of saliva and enough money to pay for a simple genetic test, and it can tell them whether they carry the mutant gene.

Genespeak
Human Genome Project – a project designed to analyse every gene in the genetic blueprint of a human.
Genome – the complete collection of genes that an organism carries on its chromosomes.

A massive, multi-billion dollar research programme to find, map and analyse every gene in the genetic blueprint for a human is under way. Known as The Human Genome Project, it will eventually allow people to be tested for scores of genetic defects.

The day may soon arrive when some people will be able to plan their futures on the basis of genetic tests that they take early in life.

Are you a carrier?

➤About three in every hundred people carry the mutant gene for cystic fibrosis, but won't develop the disease, because they're heterozygous – they carry a copy of the normal gene on a matching chromosome.

If you're someone like this, who carries a recessive mutation hidden behind a normal dominant gene, your problems start if you decide to have children with a partner who has a similar arrangement of genes. If you suspect the gene might be present in your family, you can consult a genetic counsellor, who advises patients what the risks might be.

And if you take a test and find that you are both carriers of the gene, you can calculate what the odds are that your child will inherit the disease. It's easy for cystic fibrosis, which is caused by a single mutant gene: every time you have a child, there'll be a one in four chance that it will inherit both copies of the gene and develop the disease.

Dare you risk it?

➤So people who plan to have children can choose to take a genetic test, to see if either partner carries a chromosome with a mutant gene which causes a genetic disease like cystic fibrosis. If both partners find that they have a copy of the cystic fibrosis gene, then they know they'll have a one in four chance of having a disabled child. Dare they risk having children? This is the kind of agonizing decision that our knowledge of genetics forces us to take.

Fortunately, there are people who can help with decisions like this. Genetic counsellors discuss all the options and possible outcomes with patients. But the ultimate, difficult decisions will always lie with people who carry the defective genes.

People who come from families with a history of particular genetic diseases are more likely to be carriers of hidden, recessive copies of the genes, so they're the ones who'll be most likely to want to take the tests. Would you take a genetic test to see if you are a carrier of a genetic disease? Most polls carried out so far suggest that most people don't want to know.

A 1996 poll in clinics in Nashville Tennessee invited people to take a free test for cystic fibrosis. Over 125,000 people visited the clinics where the test was offered but only 238 people asked for more information. And only 179 – less that 0.15 per cent of people who visited the clinic – offered to have their finger pricked for the blood sample that would reveal the tell-tale result.

People gave all sorts of reasons for not wanting to take the test. Many feared that they wouldn't be able to get health insurance (to pay for medical treatment) if they were found to carry the disease. Some were against the test on religious grounds, believing that God had decided their fate and they should not interfere.

There have been similar findings in Europe. It seems that people aren't ready for genetic testing yet, and it's not hard to see why. Once they know that they carry a genetic defect, they will need to make some difficult decisions.

'When the [cystic fibrosis] gene was identified, people were very enthusiastic about screening, but it turns out that seven years later they don't want it.'
(Lap-Chee Tsui, one of the discoverers of the most common gene causing cystic fibrosis)

Last chance

➤So imagine that you and your partner take a test and both prove to be carriers of a serious genetic defect – far worse than cystic fibrosis, for example. You decide to take a calculated risk and have a child.

Then you discover that you have been unlucky. The doctors tell you that your child will be born with terrible genetic disabilities and will probably be in constant pain. They warn you that it will probably need constant care and attention, every minute of the day. They tell you that it might be best for you and the child if the embryo was aborted.

A developing baby is called an embryo until it's eight weeks old. After that it's called a foetus. Embryos that are growing in a mother's womb can be tested, to see what genes they carry. If they have mutant genes that make it certain that they will be born with a severe genetic disease, then their parents can decide to have the embryo aborted.

As Martin and Paula discovered, this is a terrible decision to be faced with. Martin, who knew that a serious genetic defect ran in his family, takes up the story:

'We couldn't believe it at first, when doctors told us that our child would be born so severely handicapped. You see, we desperately wanted a baby. We knew there was a risk, but we just hoped that we'd be lucky, and that our child would be born fit and well. It was an agonizing decision, but in the end, we took the doctor's advice and went ahead with the abortion. But I still wonder to this day whether we did the right thing.'

The decision to abort a developing human embryo or foetus is a terrible one to have to make. Sometimes genetic tests for major, severe birth defects are only offered to parents who agree in advance to an abortion if the embryo or foetus is found to be defective.

But who is really qualified to decide which genetically defective embryos are too severely handicapped to be allowed to survive?

The quest for perfection

➤Every mother wants a perfect baby. And yet, almost every week, geneticists discover new mutant genes in the human DNA molecule that seem to be responsible for differences in human development.

Every year, about 30,000 children are born in Europe with inherited genetic diseases that will kill them. Thousands more are disabled, or suffer health problems that can ruin their lives.

Besides genes that cause major, life-threatening diseases, many other genes have been found that are believed to affect dyslexia, diabetes, alcoholism, schizophrenia, sexuality, bad behaviour and intelligence.

In most cases, what has really been discovered is that people who fit one of these descriptions tend to have a particular gene more often than people who don't fit the description. Sometimes scientists have found a particular gene that runs in families where several people show one of these characteristics. But this means that there is only circumstantial evidence that genes are the cause. There is no proof that a gene causes the characteristics.

So where should we draw the line? Should we consider aborting embryos that carry a gene that might make them develop violent behaviour later in life? Could the day come when only embryos that conform to our ideas of a 'perfect' person are allowed to survive? All this new knowledge presents us with the problem of deciding what, if anything, should be done with it.

Listen to some of the arguments:

Who can say what a 'perfect' person should be like? Who has the right to decide what's normal or abnormal? Is there anyone who's perfect enough themselves to make a decision like that?

But if we could screen out embryos that have genes for some kinds of undesirable behaviour we could build a society without 'defects'. We could reduce crime and violence, and save society from a lot of unnecessary expense.

And where would you draw the line between embryos that you'd abort and embryos that you'd allow to be born? Would you concentrate on eliminating the 'worst' people, or would you only let the best, most intelligent people be born?

Well, you've got to admit that the world might be a better place if we had more intelligent people and fewer people that were criminal or antisocial.

There have been some very intelligent criminals. So what would you do if you found an embryo that had genes for high intelligence *and* criminal behaviour?

And don't forget that some of the world's greatest artists and scientists have been severely disabled, alcoholic, mentally unstable or have outraged society with their behaviour.

'If you could find the gene which determines sexuality and a woman decides she doesn't want a homosexual child, well, let her.'

Professor James D. Watson, co-discoverer of the structure of the DNA molecule, in a 1997 interview in the *Sunday Telegraph* newspaper. In the interview he argued that the decision to abort a foetus that has been tested should be made by a mother, not by society. He also argued that it was the moral responsibility of parents to ensure that their babies were born as healthy as possible.

A weighty problem

➤Could the day come when only embryos that conform to our ideas of a 'perfect' person survive? It might depend on what we class as 'perfect'.

Recently, two genes have been discovered in mice that seem to affect the way they put on weight.

One, called the ob gene (for obesity), gives mice an insatiable appetite. They can't stop eating. The other gene, called tub (for tubby), makes them pile on the pounds even when they eat normal amounts of food.

Suppose we could screen for these genes in human embryos. We live in a society which is obsessed with weight-watching and ultra-slim cover-girl bodies. Would some mothers prefer not to give birth to children endowed with the ob and tub genes?

Genespeak

Artificial insemination – a laboratory technique where a mother's egg is fertilized by a father's sperm in a test tube. Then the fertilized embryo is implanted in the mother's womb. This technique is often used when couples have difficulty conceiving a child, because the father is infertile. The sperm is supplied by an anonymous sperm donor.

It does seem that, given a choice, some parents would like to be able to design babies to their own specification. In America and Europe artificial insemination clinics already try to select sperm from sperm donors whose skin, eye and hair colours match those of the parents, so there will be no clue that the child's biological father is really an anonymous donor.

It has been possible for some time to know the sex of a baby before birth. Some experiments show that it may eventually be possible to decide in advance whether you want a boy or girl, by artificially inseminating eggs with sperm that will produce either a male or female baby, according to the parents' choice.

In some poor countries parents want sons, not daughters, because sons have more opportunity to work and earn money, while parents have to pay for daughters' marriages. In China, where sons are preferred in poor families, infanticide has been practised in rural areas in recent years, although the law forbids it. Thousands of female babies have been killed at birth.

There are those who say that new genetic engineering techniques have brought the day of the perfect, 'designer' baby one step closer. They also fear that we might see the return of a strategy for 'improving' the human race, which arose during a shameful period in human history in the 1930s.

The road to genocide

> ***Genespeak***
> ***Eugenics* – *a movement started in Britain designed to improve the 'genetic health' of the population by eliminating genes for sloth, idleness and irresponsibility and encouraging thrift, intelligence and hard work. There was, of course, no evidence that genes were responsible for any of these characteristics.***

➤In the 1930s a movement called eugenics became popular, led by people who believed that the human race could be 'improved' by encouraging marriages between highly intelligent, physically 'perfect' people.

Eugenicists believed that 'defective' genes could be removed from the population by preventing people who carried them from having children. Some of the grim details of what was done have only recently emerged. Thousands of people who were mentally ill, or judged to have low intelligence, were sterilized in several countries, including the United States, Canada, Norway, Denmark and Sweden, so that they couldn't pass on their defective genes by having children.

The whole programme of eugenics was doomed to failure before it began, because somewhere, amongst the tens of thousands of genes strung out along our chromosomes, every one of us carries some defective, recessive genes that are hidden behind normal dominant genes. There is no possible way of removing them all. Even if that were possible, the effect wouldn't last. Genes mutate to produce new defects all the time. This process can't be stopped.

But before the eugenics movement finally died out, it perpetrated the greatest atrocity in human history – the death camps of Nazi Germany. There, millions of people who were classified as undesirable, either because they carried defective genes or because they came from races that had a particularly high incidence of certain genes, were exterminated.

This was genocide – the destruction of people because of the genes they happened to be born with.

> ***'Where love, compassion, altruism and justice have failed, genetic manipulation will not succeed.'***
> ***(Gina Maranto, science journalist, writing about the possibility of using genetic engineering techniques to produce better human beings, 1996)***

Back to the future

➤There are some people who believe that our new knowledge of genetics, which allows us to find defective genes in people with relative ease, is leading us back towards a modern, subtle form of eugenics.

We are walking a fine line.

Today, when embryos and foetuses are aborted because they will be born with awful disabilities, it's often done because their birth would cause terrible anguish and hardship to parents who would have to care for a handicapped child twenty-four hours a day, for their whole life. The health and welfare of the mother is usually the first concern, together with the quality of life that the disabled child might enjoy. These are basic humanitarian principles.

But would it ever be right to decide who should be born on the basis of the financial costs of caring for the disabled or in a futile attempt to remove defective genes from the population, so that disabled people become less of a problem in the future? If recent research turns out to be right, it may well be a strategy that some people will support.

In 1993 the Chinese government passed a law designed to 'improve the quality of the new-born population'. Couples must be tested for hereditary mental and physical diseases before they marry. If they test positive, they may not be allowed to marry, or may be forced to be sterilized. Chinese women carrying embryos with serious genetic defects must have abortions. No one seems sure what the Chinese government means by 'a serious genetic defect'.

One of the most worrying aspects of the Chinese law is that Western genetic engineering companies are selling technology to the Chinese government that will allow them to pursue their eugenics policies.

> ***'Exporting genetic know-how to a regime that sanctions eugenics is about as morally wholesome as selling semtex [explosive] to countries that sanction terrorism.'***
> ***Editorial*, New Scientist, *16 November 1996***

Natural born killers

➤In October 1993 Dutch scientists announced that they had found a gene that might be linked to violence and antisocial behaviour in a single large family. Violent men in the family were unable to produce a vital enzyme in their nervous system.

It had already been discovered that mice with similar damaged genes are unusually aggressive. The researchers suggested that this gene might be the cause of aggression in the Dutch family.

American lawyers quickly tried to exploit this information in court.

In 1995 lawyers defending Stephen Mobley, who was accused of shooting a pizza parlour cashier during a robbery, appealed against a murder charge because Mobley suffered from a genetic imbalance in his brain chemistry.

The lawyers said he was a 'natural born killer', and that wasn't his fault. It was an accident of nature. The appeal was thrown out.

If the appeal had been upheld it would have opened the floodgates to appeals against criminal convictions on the basis of dubious genetic evidence. It would have thrown the law into turmoil.

If a gene for a 'natural born killer' did exist, the murderer would be almost as much of a victim as the person who was murdered, and worthy of automatic sympathy for being born with the disability.

When the suspicion was announced that genes for characteristics like criminality and aggression might exist, there were immediate demands from some people for these genes to be eliminated from the population. If the genes could be diagnosed in embryos, maybe these could be aborted and society could avoid the problem of having to deal with undesirable people.

It's an argument that finds strong support amongst people who like to deny that there are social causes of crime, like unemployment, bad housing and poverty. They are enthusiastic about the idea that it would be simpler and cheaper to get rid of problem people, rather than struggling to cure the social causes of crime.

'Why spend good money on people with bad genes?' they argue.

There's little scientific evidence to support this argument. Almost all scientists agree that, if there are genes that govern criminal behaviour (and this is by no means certain), then they only play a minor role in the way that people turn out. The environment is far more important.

But the very idea that genes might exist that influence bad behaviour always rouses calls from a minority of extremists for eugenic solutions.

Who should decide?

➤So how do we decide what genetic disabilities are severe enough to demand abortion?

The decision is usually based on whether the quality of life of the affected child, and of the parents who will be responsible for looking after it, will be unbearably awful.

This might be relatively straightforward in the worst cases, but how can you tell what goes on in the mind of a severely disabled person? Inside, they may have a degree of happiness that couldn't be guessed at just by looking at their outward appearance.

Genespeak
Down's syndrome – an inherited disorder caused by a chromosome defect. Sufferers are mentally retarded and physically disabled.

Martha is 19. A happy, friendly teenager who is well known to just about everyone in the small town where she lives and works. She has a job in the local baker's shop, enjoys the cinema and is adored by children at the local Sunday school where she teaches. Martha has brought immeasurable happiness into the lives of many people around her. She has the kind of life that many lonely people might envy.

Yet Martha was born with Down's syndrome, a genetic condition where she has inherited an extra chromosome. She looks different from other girls of her age, has difficulty in talking and she has disabilities which mean that she needs a lot of help with tasks that most of us wouldn't think twice about. Sadly, her disability means that she won't live as long as most of us.

We can only guess how Martha might feel if she knew that her condition is considered to be a valid reason for abortion. But it's people like her who lead others to argue that we should spend more time studying the lives of genetically disabled people and consulting them, before we decide whether the potentially disabled have a right to be born.

Their point of view was best summed up in 1949 by a geneticist called Lionel Penrose, who believed that the best measure of a society's health was its willingness to provide adequate care for the people who are unable to care for themselves.

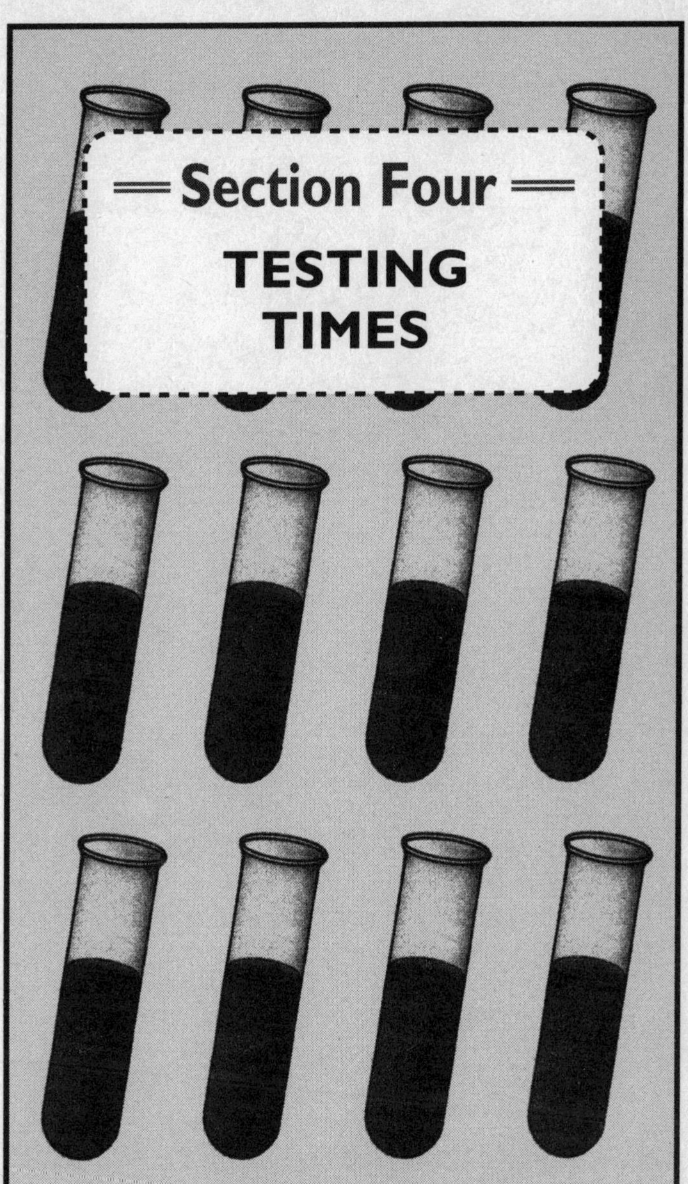
Section Four
TESTING TIMES

Agonizing decisions

➤Improving knowledge of DNA means that scientists are constantly finding new mutant genes that are involved in genetic disabilities. Genes have been discovered for colon cancer, Huntington's chorea, heart disease and Alzheimer's disease. And tests are now becoming available for people who want to find out whether they've inherited these.

Genespeak
Colon cancer – cancerous growths in parts of the large intestine.
Huntington's chorea – a disease which causes jerky movements in the sufferer that they can't control. They gradually become demented.
Alzheimer's disease – a brain disease, which causes gradual loss of memory.
Oncology – the study of cancerous diseases.

As we've already seen, testing people to see whether they carry genes for defects that they'll never suffer from, but which they might pass on to their children, can be useful – even if it does leave parents with some heart-rending decisions.

But when a positive test for a defect tells a patient that they're likely to develop a life-threatening disease themselves later in life, the decisions are even tougher. This is a problem faced by thousands of women who carry genes that make it more likely that they'll develop breast cancer, which is one of the biggest killers of women. Some forms of the disease are inherited.

In 1994 scientists discovered a defective gene called BRCA1 which can be one of the causes of a kind of breast cancer in women who inherit the disease from their parents. 85 per cent of women who carry this faulty gene go on to develop the disease. Some also develop cancers in their ovaries. Recently, a second breast cancer gene, BRCA2, has been identified.

For $2400 a private genetics company in Virginia in the United States will test women to see if they carry a defective BRCA1 and BRCA2 gene. If they test positive, it means that they know that they are likely, but not certain, to develop a disease that they can't prevent. There is no treatment yet that will stop it happening.

One advantage of knowing that they have the gene is that they can check for symptoms – small lumps in their breast tissues – regularly. Early detection means that these can be removed quickly, before the cancerous growths spread, and this greatly increases a woman's chance of survival. But there's nothing she can do to ensure that she never develops the cancer, except to have her perfectly healthy breasts and ovaries removed. That means that she can't develop the disease, but there is always the possibility that she might never have developed cancer anyway.

'All individuals at hereditary risk from cancer should have access to appropriate genetic testing.'
(American Society of Clinical Oncology)

The test presents women with terrible dilemmas. Imagine the questions that might race through the mind of a young mother who tests positive.

'Should I have surgery? If I don't, I'll have to live the rest of my life in constant fear of the strong possibility that I'll get breast cancer, that might kill me.'

'Have I already passed this gene on to my daughter? It

makes me feel guilty, even though there's nothing I could have done to prevent it. Should I have my daughter tested? If I do, she'll have to grow up with the same terrible anxieties.'

'I'm pregnant. Should I have the foetus tested? If the test is positive, would it be better if the child wasn't born? Perhaps I should have an abortion.'

'What if I go ahead and have another child who carries the gene – will she blame me for passing on my problem to her, when I knew she would be affected?'

What began as a simple health check becomes a situation where a woman has to make life and death decisions. No wonder that many people believe that providing an easily accessible commercial service for life and death information like this shouldn't be allowed.

In 1996 Jeremy Rifkin, a famous campaigner who opposes many uses of the new genetic technologies, founded a campaign to block moves that would make testing of breast cancer commercially possible. He described it as 'the first genetic rights movement in history' and is backed by women's rights activists from 250 organizations in 68 countries.

'Our view is that this test is a cynical development which will profit the testing companies concerned but provide no medical benefits to women. They instead will be worried witless by being told they may develop a disease which they cannot prevent.' (Julie Sheppard, The Genetics Forum)

There are feminist organizations who say that Rifkin and his allies are wrong. They support genetic testing for breast cancer genes as a commercial activity because they believe that the profits that it generates, and the potential human suffering that it reveals, will help to support and stimulate research which will eventually discover cures for the disease.

> ***'There is always a concern that the promise of fat dividends for shareholders is a major driving force behind any company's involvement in the health field.'***
> ***(Editorial,* Nature, *1996)***

As with almost every issue in the world of genetics, there are contrasting viewpoints about how the new scientific discoveries should be used.

Could you take the strain?

➤So would you take a genetic test that might reveal that you carried an unsuspected genetic defect, that will end your life early? Here are some possible outcomes that you might consider, before you make a decision:

☐ You take the test as part of a routine health check and find no defects. You're lucky. No worries.

☐ You read in the newspaper that the test is available. You think you might carry the defect. Eventually, after months – maybe years – of anxiety, you finally decide to take a test, expecting the worst. No abnormalities are detected. It leaves you feeling that you have wasted your time worrying in the first place.

☐ You feel fit and healthy when you take the test. You expect good news, but find out that you have a gene for an incurable disease that will probably kill you in middle age.

The last scenario is the worst one. How you react will depend on your personality. You might:

☐ shrug your shoulders and decide to make the best of the rest of your life. You know roughly how much time you've got, so you can live the remainder of your life to the full and put all your affairs in order before you die;
or
☐ plunge into the depths of despair, knowing that you are consigned to early disability or death, with nothing that you can do about it. The bad news blights the rest of your life.

It's obvious that once people have access to this kind of information, then they'll need to be able to call on support from counsellors, to help them deal with bad news.

'We are in an interim state of being able to spot victims but not help them . . . Great care and effort in counselling will be needed, and that will require investment. Some people will simply want to know the worst, to arrange their affairs properly.'
(Dr Simon Lovestone, Alzheimer's disease genetics consortium)

'Alzheimer's disease, which leads to loss of memory and senile dementia, usually affects the elderly. But a few people carry a rare mutant gene that gives them a 50 per cent chance of developing Alzheimer's disease in middle age. When Swedish scientists developed a test that told a young woman that she carried the disease and would develop Alzheimer's in her 50s, the knowledge drove her to the brink of suicide.'
(Reported in* The Observer *newspaper, 1995)

Uninsurable, unemployable

➤There are other aspects of genetic testing that can ruin people's lives. It could destroy your employment prospects and make it difficult for you to insure your life and health.

This could happen in several ways:

☐ You apply for a job, but your potential employers insist that you have a medical examination before they offer you the job. The examination includes a genetic test, which shows that you have a gene that will disable you in later life. Even though you are in perfect health now, they don't want problems from disabled employees in the future, so you don't get the job.

☐ You decide to apply for health insurance. This means that you make monthly payments now to a company that will pay for expensive medical treatment in the future, if you are unlucky enough to become ill. But they insist that you have a genetic test, which shows that you have a gene that means you are more likely to develop cancer later in life, although this is far from certain. The insurance company decides that they don't want to risk having to pay out for expensive treatment. They refuse to insure you.

☐ You apply for life insurance. This means that you make monthly payments and the company will pay a large sum of money to your family if you die young, so that they won't suffer hardship. But they won't insure you without a genetic test, which you fail. It turns out that you have a gene that increases the chance that you'll die from heart disease while you're still young. It's more likely that they'll have to pay out, so they demand much larger monthly premiums, which you can't afford. So now you'll be uninsured if you die young, and your family will suffer.

In every case, you are being discriminated against because of genes that you were unlucky enough to be born with. Through no fault of your own, you are being denied access to rights and services that are automatic to less unlucky people.

No wonder many people are worried about what happens to information from genetic testing. If it ends up in the wrong hands, it could ruin your life. So in many parts of the world governments are grappling with the problem of genetic discrimination.

> ***'The idea that there will be a huge databank of genetic information on millions of people is repulsive.'***
> ***(James D. Watson, co-discoverer of the structure of DNA)***

Such discrimination against more familiar physical disabilities, like blindness, paraplegia or thalidomide victims, would be outlawed in America, Europe and in many other parts of the world. The jury is still out on how best to protect the rights of citizens against misuse of genetic screening results. Finding ways of keeping this information confidential is one of the first priorities.

> ***'Employers and insurance companies will be biased against women who have tested positive for breast cancer genes.'***
> ***(Vandana Shiva, President, The Research Foundation for Science, Technology and Natural Resource Policy, New Delhi, India)***

Try this test

➤You want to have children? Should you take a genetic test, to see whether you have any hidden genetic defects? Which of the factors below would most influence your decision? Put them in numbered order, then compare your list with the results of a survey of the American public, which is printed upside down, underneath.

☐ There's a risk that you'll have to live the rest of your life with the knowledge that you are a carrier of a genetic defect.

☐ There are lots of complicated forms to fill out.

☐ If you test positive, it might mean that you have to decide whether any future children should be aborted during pregnancy.

☐ It might mean that you'll be denied life insurance.

☐ You'll only take the test if your doctor advises you to.

☐ You'll do whatever your marriage partner decides.

☐ The test costs money. Is it worth paying for it?

☐ You'll need to give a blood sample.

This is how the American public ranked these considerations:

1 *Ability to get life insurance.*
2 *Risk of being a carrier.*
3 *Partner's opinion*
4 *Fear of having to have an abortion.*
5 *Doctor's opinion*
6 *Cost*
7 *Don't like having blood samples taken.*
8 *Too many forms to fill out.*

Ultimately the decision to take genetic tests that might change the course of our lives is a personal choice, but before taking a test it might be wise to bear in mind some recent genetic research.

In December 1996 researchers at the United States Institute of Mental Health announced that they had found a gene which played a part in determining whether people are cheerful and optimistic by nature, or anxious and pessimistic. The gene seems to influence the way the brain reacts to molecules inside it, so affecting mood.

Perhaps, before being tested for anything else, we should find out which version of this gene we carry. It might determine how we'll react to bad news.

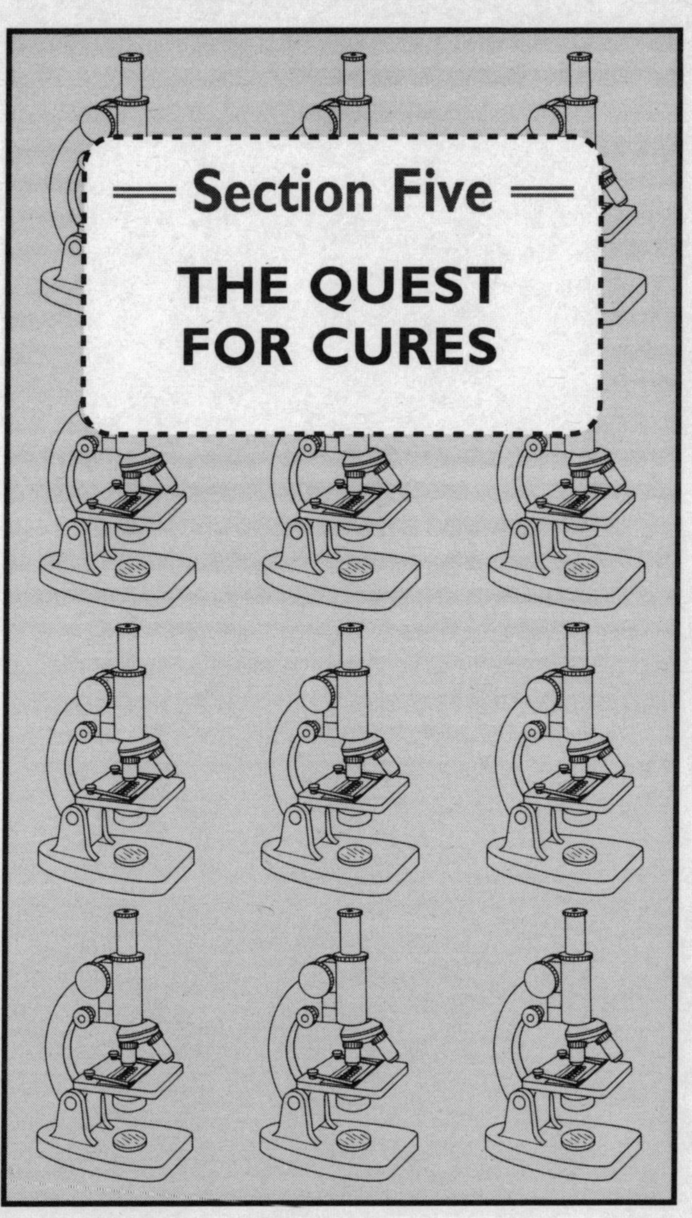

Section Five

THE QUEST FOR CURES

Gene therapy

Genespeak
Therapy – treatment of medical disorders that doesn't involve surgery.
Therapeutic – something that's effective in treating medical disorders.

➤In the long term, scientists need to be able to find defective genes on chromosomes before they can hope to develop cures for the diseases that they cause. This is one reason why there is a major international effort under way – called the Human Genome Project – to map all the genes that make up a human being. It will help scientists to locate defective genes, find out why they don't work properly, and devise drugs or other treatments to defeat them.

But treatments and cures are likely to take a long time to arrive.

The favourite technique for developing treatments that will combat genetic diseases is known as gene therapy. The basic idea behind gene therapy is that healthy copies of genes are introduced into the patient's cells, counteracting the defective genes that cause the disease. In the early days it was hoped that these treatments might advance quickly, but so far they have not been very successful.

Firstly, it's not easy to deliver the extra genes to the right part of the body. In one promising therapy for cystic fibrosis, which is being developed at Oxford University, the genes are delivered to the lungs inside fatty droplets called liposomes, which are sprayed in through the patient's nose. The liposomes join up with lung cells and release a healthy copy of the gene in the place where it's needed. In tests in

1996 the treatment worked in half the patients with no harmful side effects, but the benefits don't seem to last long.

Side effects are a constant worry in gene therapy. There are several reasons why gene therapy can go wrong.

Every cell in our bodies contains the same genes, but they aren't all active at the same time. Some are only 'switched on' in particular organs, where they have special tasks. They're 'turned off' everywhere else.

So it's vital that genes that are inserted into us in gene therapy are targeted to the right cells, where they're only switched on at the right moment. A therapeutic gene for cystic fibrosis needs to be switched on in the lungs, not in the brain tissues, where it might cause terrible damage.

Taming deadly viruses

➤Some researchers are using an alternative strategy. They're developing viruses that can enter defective cells and equip them with healthy DNA. Viruses naturally infect cells when they cause diseases, using their host's DNA to help make copies of themselves. Viruses can be genetically engineered to become harmless delivery systems for useful genes, but there are many hazards to overcome, as recent tests have shown.

Parkinson's disease and Alzheimer's disease both slowly destroy the nervous system, so scientists in the United States have tried to develop a virus that will shuttle replacement genes into the brain. In tests with rats, it seems to work if it's injected directly into the brain. But if the virus is injected anywhere else in the body – like the rat's foot, for instance – it causes severe brain inflammation. The immune system in the rat's brain puts up a fight, to keep the virus out.

Problems like this mean that gene therapy is still a long way from becoming a regular medical treatment. But genetic engineers are constantly coming up with novel solutions. The most alarming suggestion is to deliver replacement genes to defective cells in a weakened strain of the HIV virus, which in its normal form often leads patients to develop AIDS.

One of the things that makes HIV such an effective disease is that it's very good at smuggling itself into cells and chromosomes. A modified form of the virus might be an ideal delivery system for carrying replacement genes into defective cells. Genetic engineers would need to delete genes that enable the virus to multiply inside its host and cause damage, and replace them with a cargo of therapeutic genes that they wanted the virus to carry into the target cells.

But, as the scientists say, 'the real challenge will be to convince the public that HIV could be a safe medical tool.'

Cancer cell suicide

Genespeak
Prodrug – drugs that are activated by the cancer cells that they're designed to destroy.

➤An even more imaginative technique for treating tumours is to develop therapies which are harmless to normal cells and are only activated by cancer tumour cells. The Cancer Research Campaign and the drug company Glaxo Wellcome are developing a virus which carries genes which are only switched on when the virus arrives in cancer cells, making the tumour cells commit suicide. The virus, known as a prodrug, doesn't become active until it meets a cancer cell. It looks promising: tumours in mice shrunk by up to 90 per cent when they were treated with it.

Who pays?

➤There is a catch to these scientific advances that no one has really tackled yet.

Gene therapy treatments will cost money – probably a great deal of money. Countries like Britain, with a public National Health Service that struggles to find enough money to finance existing cures, will need to raise more money through taxes to finance these high-tech treatments. Will public health services be able to afford to provide expensive new gene therapies for everyone who needs them? Or will people be asked to take out extra health insurance, to pay for treatments if they're unlucky enough to need them?

In many other countries citizens rely on private health insurance to pay for medical treatment. The constant discovery of ways to locate and treat human diseases is bound to make health insurance more expensive, because it will mean that insurance policies will have to face the possibility of paying for treatment for costly cures.

Eventually, access to many forms of gene therapy might only be available to those who can afford to take out health insurance to pay for them. The monthly health insurance payments by people who have taken genetic tests that show that they'll need this kind of therapy are likely to be extremely high.

If access to gene therapy depends on wealth, it could become the preserve of the privileged few. And in the worst cases some individuals – and perhaps whole families, including their unborn children – could be uninsurable, because of the high cost of treating their inherited defect.

Could this lead to a two-layered society, divided into a wealthy, healthy élite who have access to genetic therapy and a poor underclass who can't afford these services? This is a serious problem, created by modern advances in medical science, that politicians and economists will have to consider.

But, for now at least, gene therapy is still only a distant but promising prospect. In future, some people will always have to live with the knowledge that they harbour genetic diseases, long before therapies are found to treat them.

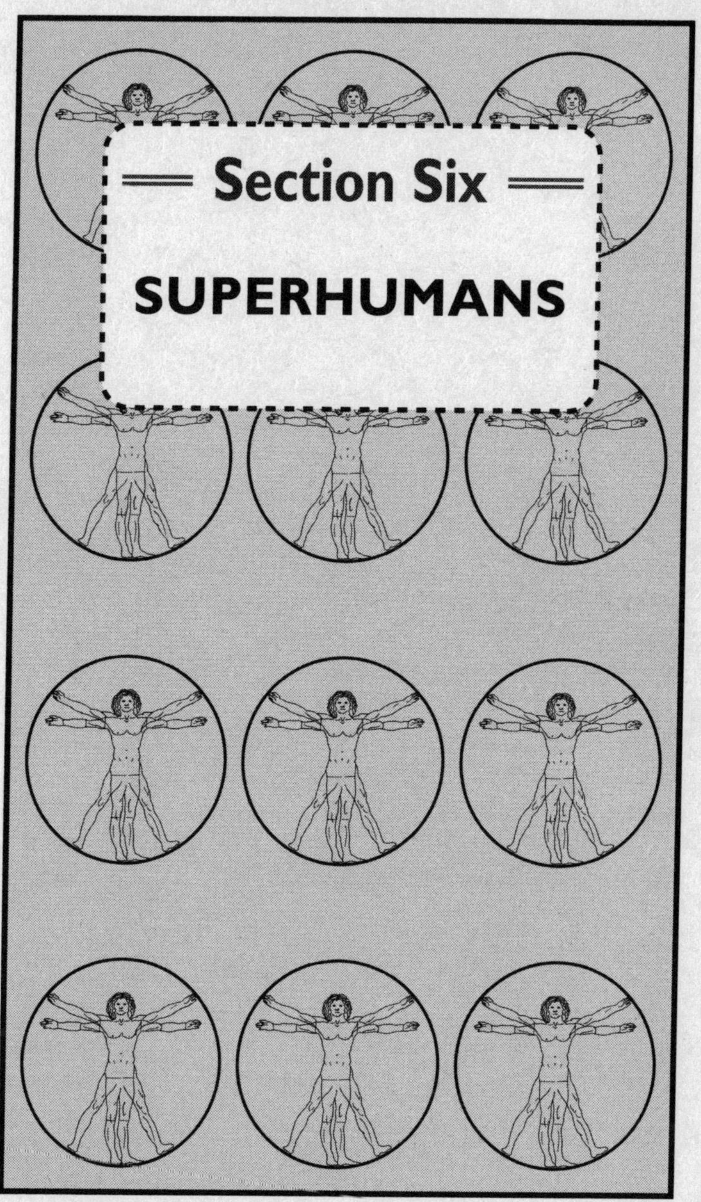
Section Six
SUPERHUMANS

My dad was a pig

➤In 1996 US scientists at the University of Pennsylvania and the University of Texas revealed results of an astonishing experiment that showed that it might be possible for human sperm cells to be genetically manipulated, stored and used indefinitely to produce modified people.

Sperm cells are produced by cells called stem cells in the testies. The scientists developed a laboratory culture of rat stem cells that kept dividing and lived indefinitely in a culture dish in a refrigerator. They didn't produce sperm there, though. For that the scientists had to take a few stem cells and transplant them back into a testis of a rat.

Then they discovered that they could even transplant rat stem cells into the testis of a mouse, which would produce rat sperm. It seems likely that rat stem cells might make sperm in the testis of any mammal that they're transplanted into.

Understandably, this startling research attracted the interest of journalists, who began to wonder just where research like this might be leading.

'Could it be,' they asked, 'that with a bit of tinkering, it might be possible to get human stem cells working inside the testes of another mammal?'

Scientists generally don't like to speculate on questions like this, but they had to admit that, yes, it might well be possible. The rat-to-mouse experiment suggested that you can go across species barriers. If you wanted to do this with human stem cells, it might be easiest to put the human cells in a pig's testis.

The scientists who did the experiments were only interested in the scientific principles involved, but people who are less cautious than scientists are prone to let their imaginations run away with them. What if we could get pigs to produce human sperm? What would be the use of such an experiment?

Imagine this scenario.

Suppose scientists took some human stem cells and, with the help of genetic engineering, deleted genetic defects that led to diseases, or maybe added combinations of genes that would improve behaviour, intelligence or any other characteristics that they considered desirable.

Then they grew the stem cells in a sterile culture, where they could be kept alive at low temperatures indefinitely.

When sperm was needed, the stem cells were transplanted into pig testes. Then the pigs would produce human sperm carrying all the desirable characteristics. This could be used to fertilize human eggs, to produce embryos that could be implanted into women, where they would develop into genetically modified babies.

Some of the technology for doing this already exists. Women whose husbands are infertile and cannot have children by normal means often have eggs implanted in them that were originally fertilized by a donor's sperm in a test tube.

So the culture of stem cells in the refrigerator, with a little help from a pig, could give rise to generations of genetically modified humans. Once the first of these superhumans grew up, they would pass on the genetic improvements in their own sperm or egg cells, producing families of modified people.

This isn't so far-fetched. Scientists are already working on a similar strategy for producing more productive farm animals. It's called germ line therapy.

In gene therapy the defects in a genetically disabled person are modified during their lifetime and are not passed on to future generations.

In germ line therapy, people's reproductive cells are altered, so all their descendants inherit the change once it has been made.

Germ line therapy is considered to be forbidden territory for scientists to wander into. It could be used to breed a 'master race'. Using genetic screening and gene therapy to reduce human suffering conforms to the highest ideals of the medical profession. Using the same technology to design 'better' people takes medicine into territory where most scientists fear to tread.

But there is another method of building a master race. It's called cloning, and that too is already well advanced.

Cloning people

➤In plants the best varieties can be multiplied by taking cuttings. To make an exact copy – or clone – of a geranium, all you need to do is cut off a piece of stem and stick it in some soil. The cutting will form new roots and become an exact copy of the original plant.

Animals rarely multiply by making clones of themselves. Instead they reproduce sexually. One of the consequences of this is that every individual in the population is slightly different.

For a long time, animal breeders have wanted to make exact copies – clones – of the most productive farm animals. It would be extremely useful, and very lucrative, if we could make endless copies of the cows that produced the most milk, or the sheep that grew the best wool.

Recently, scientists have succeeded in cloning sheep.

On 23 February, 1997 researchers at the Roslin Institute in Scotland hit the headlines when they announced that they had developed a way to clone sheep.

It took 277 attempts but finally their first successful clone, called Dolly, made her debut to the world's press and instantly becoming the most photographed sheep in history.

She was created by first extracting a nucleus (the information centre of a cell, containing DNA) from her mother's mammary gland, then using this nucleus to replace the nucleus in one of her mother's eggs and then finally reimplanting the egg in her mother's womb. After that, Dolly grew like any other embryo and was born in the usual way.

Dolly is an exact genetic copy of her mother. She has no father. She has been grown from parts of just two of her mother's cells. The technique that created her paves the way for producing whole flocks of identical cloned sheep from just one individual that has been genetically manipulated to produce commercially valuable products, such as medicines, in their milk.

There's no reason in principle why this technique shouldn't be used to clone people. The scientists who cloned Dolly claimed that they could clone humans within two years, if they were given the money and the resources they needed. Their announcement set off a wave of speculation in the press about the potential benefits of human cloning. Suggestions included:

☐ Cloning babies who died in infancy, so that grief-stricken mothers could have an exact replacement copy of their child.

☐ Cloning spare copies of people, so that their clones could be used for spare part surgery. The clone's organs could be used for transplants later in life, when the body of the original person that the clone came from began to wear out. This would solve the problem of shortage of organs for transplants for once and for all. When your body began to wear out or deteriorate, you could fit a replacement part grown from one of your cloned embryos, without fear of rejection of the part by your immune system.

Some observers even declared men would soon be redundant, because sex would no longer be needed to create babies. The world could be populated by females, cloned from their own cells.

Cloned people would be different individuals with different personalities – just like identical twins – even though they would be physically similar to the owner of the original donor cell they were created from. This is because the character of a person depends on the surroundings they grow up in, as well as the genes they inherit. A cloned daughter would look exactly like her mother, but she would grow up in a different time, in different circumstances to her parent, so her attitudes, beliefs and behaviour would be different.

Imagine being the mother of a cloned daughter. There would be a terrible temptation to try to live your life again through your clone, as you watched 'yourself' grow up, trying to prevent your clone making the same mistakes the second time around, or forcing your clone to do the things you wish you'd done. Rows are common enough between parents and their children anyway, but imagine how much worse they'd be if you were a clone whose parent saw you as another version of themselves who wasn't doing as well as they expected!

This all sounds like science fiction, but so did many other aspects of biotechnology until they suddenly became science fact. If you had told scientists in 1950 that animal genes could be transferred into plants, they would have laughed at you. Now it's being done all the time.

The United States government was so alarmed at the prospect of human cloning – especially when another research group announced that they had already cloned a monkey – that it rushed through laws banning experiments with humans. In Britain existing legislation would make it illegal, but there are other parts of the world where it could (and probably will) be done.

Eternal life

➤If people could be cloned, they might have a kind of eternal life. A constant stream of exact copies could be produced to replace them as they wore out and died.

Some scientists are already working on projects that are designed to postpone old age and death. They're on the trail of genes that slow down the ageing process. Researchers predict that the existing human life span could easily be doubled, with the help of a little genetic engineering.

Geneticists in Canada have found mutant genes in tiny eelworms that allow these creatures to live up to six times longer than normal. They slow down the rate of development of the animals, which also move more slowly, and the scientists believe that similar genes could probably exist in humans.

No human would want to be equipped with a gene like this. It would give them a childhood that lasted for 60 years and their metabolism would be so sluggish that they'd move as slowly as sloths. But several other genes have been discovered that slow down the ageing process with less drastic side effects. It seems to be only a matter of time before our knowledge of genetics increases the average human life span, from around 70 years to a century or more.

Although individuals would surely welcome a longer life, it would present all sorts of problems for governments. The proportion of older people in the population, who had retired from work, would grow. Consider the consequences:

- ☐ Would the state be able to afford to pay us retirement pensions if we lived for 70 extra years?
- ☐ Could health services afford to provide the extra medical care that would be needed if we lived longer?
- ☐ Would the increase in the total number of people alive impose an impossible strain on the world's resources?
- ☐ If people lived to 140, they might work until they were 100 years old. What effect would this have on employment for the young?
- ☐ If birth rates stayed the same, young people would be in a minority and society would be dominated by the elderly.

Modern genetics has the potential to make great changes to the society we live in. Usually, scientists get so carried away with the excitement of their work that they don't spare much time to think about its wider consequences. Usually, in the world of genetic engineering, the new technology provides us with choices before we've thought about what they really mean for our long-term future.

84 Could it happen here?

➤Cloned people? Genetically-engineered superhumans? Ridiculous! Immoral! Even if science does find ways to make it possible, society would forbid it.

Or would it?

People often forget that biotechnology and genetic engineering are now worldwide technologies, available to scientists everywhere. The basic steps are not really that difficult to master. Training can be easily bought. All the techniques are published in scientific journals. You can go to your local library and find out what you need to do to clone a sheep, although you'd need to be very well trained before you could begin. Any reasonably well-equipped laboratory, anywhere in the world, could begin a genetic engineering programme. Unlike the development of nuclear bombs, where it's very hard to get hold of the radioactive raw materials, the basic requirements for genetic engineering are available from scientific equipment and chemical suppliers.

While Europe, Australasia and America might reject these ideas for drastic tinkering with human genetics, other societies might well be tempted to try them out. There are no worldwide laws for ethical conduct in science. There are no international bodies that control what research can or can't be done. It's not difficult to imagine the attractions of these techniques to countries ruled by dynasties of dictators, who have absolute power and access to vast wealth. The prospect of extended life through cloning might be irresistible.

Even in the great democracies like America there are people who cannot face the thought of death and oblivion. They chose to have their corpses frozen in liquid nitrogen, in the hope that technology might one day find ways to revive them. There are massive commercial profits awaiting companies whose scientists can find ways to extend the human life span in any way, or move us a step closer to physical immortality.

Modern genetic engineering and cloning technology might just do that.

In June 1997 a Swiss-based religious sect began advertizing a human cloning service on the Internet. The company offers infertile or homosexual couples a child that will be cloned from one of their cells – for a charge of about $200,000.

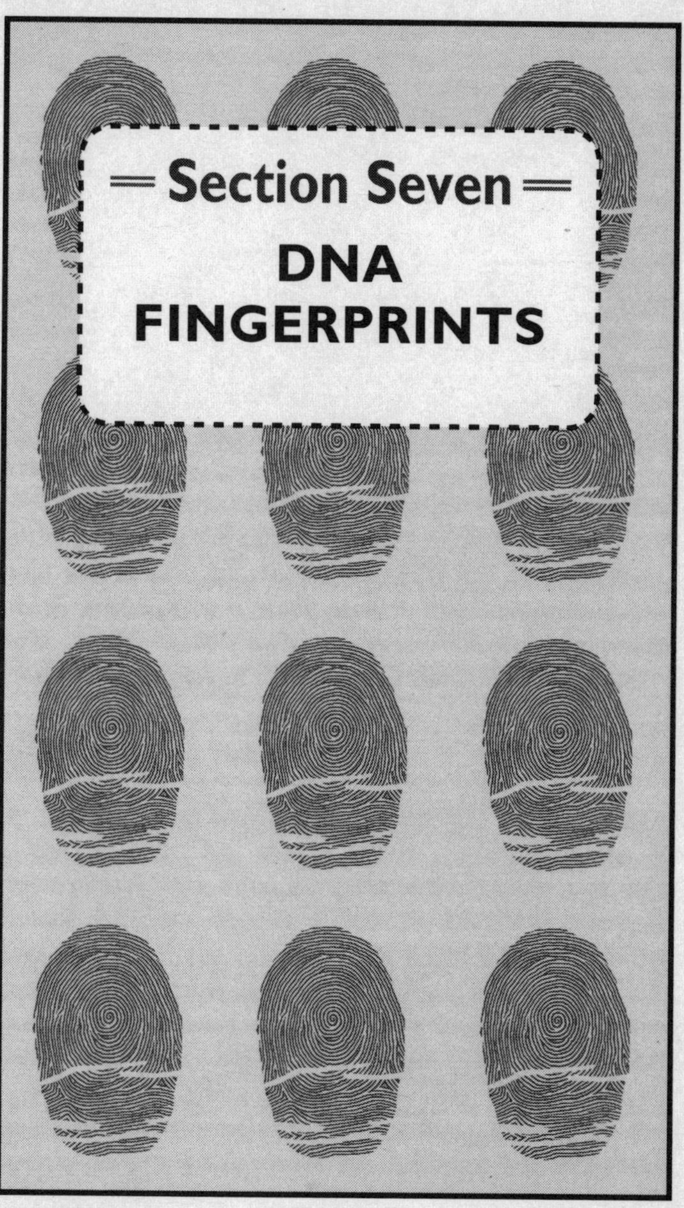

Section Seven

DNA FINGERPRINTS

The burglar and the barcode

Genespeak
***Database** – a large collection of information, arranged so that any of it can be retrieved quickly. Computers store large databases and access them in seconds.*
***DNA fingerprint** – a unique pattern, produced when fragments of a person's DNA are separated in an electric field.*

➤There was a tinkle of glass as the burglar broke a small pane of glass in the front door, reached through to turn the key that had been left in the lock, and let himself into the house. He paused for a while, listening, in case the noise had woken up the owners, but there was only silence. They were sleeping soundly upstairs.

Then he moved quickly and quietly from room to room in the house, searching drawers and cupboards, and collecting valuables. He wore gloves, to make certain that he left no fingerprints. Within a few minutes he'd made a clean getaway.

He didn't notice that he'd cut himself until he got home and began to sort through the spoils of his evening's work. It must have happened when he opened the door, by reaching through the jagged fragments of glass stuck around the edge of the broken window.

He washed the cut under the tap and didn't think any more about it, until the police arrived to take him away for questioning.

That day – 11 August 1995 – was a landmark in the history of law enforcement in the United Kingdom. Unfortunately for the burglar, the police already had genetic information that could be used to identify him, stored on a database that they'd been assembling for years. Genetic information from the blood sample matched it perfectly.

It was the first time that this technique had been used to catch a burglar.

The arrest was hailed as the greatest breakthrough in the fight against crime since 1902 – the year that saw the first use of conventional fingerprints to convict a criminal. In that year Harry Jackson, another burglar, left a thumb print that was used to convict him after he broke into a house.

The technique that caught the burglar – called DNA fingerprinting – was first developed by Professor Alec Jeffreys at Leicester University in England in 1984, using some of the techniques that make genetic engineering possible.

A sample of DNA from blood, semen, hair or body tissues of a person is cut into small pieces with enzymes. Then the fragments are separated in an electric current on a gel. The different-sized pieces move at different rates in the current and separate into a pattern of bands. The pattern looks very much like the barcode on goods in a shop. Like a barcode, it's used for identification.

Just like old-fashioned fingerprints, DNA patterns can be used to identify criminal suspects and prove that they were at the scene of the crime, by comparing samples of body tissues that they leave behind with a sample taken from their body. It doesn't need much to convict them – the skin cells clinging to the base of a hair, or a smear of blood on a piece of broken glass are enough.

> ***'The database is great news for most of us, but seriously bad news for criminals. My message to the criminal is simple: DNA can catch you . . . It will bring more criminals to justice. Equally important, it will help to eliminate innocent suspects.'***
> ***(Michael Howard, British Home Secretary, 1995)***

DNA databases

➤Police forces of many advanced nations are now building up libraries of DNA fingerprints of known criminals and suspects. These will be used to convict them if they offend again and leave tell-tale samples. So in future – even if you commit a minor traffic offence or are caught shoplifting – the police might take a DNA sample from your body and store a copy of your DNA fingerprint in a computer database. Eventually, up to five million DNA fingerprints will be stored on the computer.

In the United States the Federal Bureau of Investigation (FBI) has invested $48 million dollars in a DNA fingerprint database of criminals called CODIS – Combined DNA Index System. Police stations all over the country use this database, that can search through 17,000 DNA fingerprints per minute and check them against samples taken at the scene of the crime.

DNA profiles can do more than convict the guilty – they can also free the innocent. In August 1996 French police set free a suspect who had confessed to the rape and murder of a 13-year-old British schoolgirl called Caroline Dickinson, who had been on a school trip to France. The suspect's DNA sample showed that he could not possibly have committed the crime.

Peter Neufeld, from the United States National Association of Criminal Defence Lawyers, has estimated that if recent miscarriages of justice revealed by DNA fingerprinting are anything to go by, then at least 10 per cent of the present prison population in New York might be exonerated through this type of evidence.

Between 1991 and 1996, 36 convicted criminals on death row in the US were released on the strength of DNA evidence that proved that their convictions were unsound or that they were innocent.

But the trouble with genetic fingerprinting is that it can put innocent people in jail. Civil rights groups have pointed out all sorts of pitfalls with judgements based on genetics. Samples can be mixed up in the laboratory. They can be damaged through poor storage. Human error is always a possibility.

And there's another problem. Every person's personal DNA is unique (unless they have an identical twin), but the fingerprinting technique only analyses a small piece of the total. This is because there are three billion separate molecular 'code letters' in every person's DNA, so analysing them all would be an impossibly long and costly job.

So instead the technique just takes a small sample of their total DNA – enough to show that the probability of it being the same as someone else's is extremely remote. DNA fingerprinting only gives the probability of an exact match for a suspect's DNA sample. If the probability is sufficiently small – say one in a million – then juries will convict criminals on this evidence. But because there is no absolute certainty, civil rights campaigners believe that DNA fingerprints shouldn't be the only evidence used to convict a criminal.

> ***'To say there is just a million to one chance that the accused person is not guilty makes things sound pretty certain. But there are 50 million people in Britain, so that means there are 49 other people who could be the culprit.' (John Wadham, Director, Liberty (civil liberties watchdog), 1995)***

No more unknown soldiers

➤Many countries have a tomb of the Unknown Warrior, where the remains of a dead soldier who was too badly mutilated to be identified are buried. These nameless tombs are memorials to all the soldiers who have been killed in battle and whose remains couldn't be found or identified.

Today dead soldiers can be identified even if they are blown to pieces by artillery or burned beyond recognition. The US Department of Defence keeps compulsory DNA fingerprints of its troops, for a good but gruesome reason. It allows them to identify bits of soldiers killed in battle.

Recently, two US soldiers who refused to provide DNA samples were threatened with court martial. They saw the process as an infringement of their civil liberties, because their DNA fingerprints would be kept long after they had left the army and could be used against them in civilian life. Their profiles might have become part of a criminal investigation, alongside known criminals, even though they had never committed a crime in their life. Or the profiles might have produced information about their genes that might have led to discrimination in civilian life.

The two soldiers won their case in court. The US Army now offers to destroy DNA records of its troops when they leave military service.

The Czar's bones

➤July 1918. Ekaterinburg, Russia. A group of soldiers stand in a huddle, talking nervously to one another.

Suddenly an officer barks out an order and they stand to attention in a line. A frightened group of people – a man, his wife and his daughters – are led out of a building and lined up against a wall.

Another order. The soldiers shoulder their rifles. A volley of shots ring out, and the man and his family fall to the ground. The officer examines their bodies, ready to finish off any that might still be alive with a pistol shot. But they're all dead. He orders the bodies to be carried away and buried as quickly as possible, in an unmarked grave.

This was no ordinary execution. The soldiers have just shot Czar Nicholas II and the whole Russian royal family.

It's 1994. Times have changed in Russia, and the Communist revolution that led to the Czar's execution has run its course. Communism has been swept away.

In a laboratory a group of scientists are removing something from some human bones on a laboratory bench. The bones have come from an unmarked grave near Ekaterinburg. Could they belong to the Czar and his family? It's hard to say. An awful lot of bullet-riddled bodies were buried during the Russian revolution.

But soon the sample taken from the centre of the bones provides confirmation. It's a fragment of DNA and the scientists have been able to compare it with DNA from Czar Nicholas's living relatives, who have married into more fortunate royal families. One of these is the Duke of Edinburgh, who married the future Queen Elizabeth II of England in 1947.

Finally, three quarters of a century after their execution, the remains of Russia's last royal family can be now reburied with due reverence.

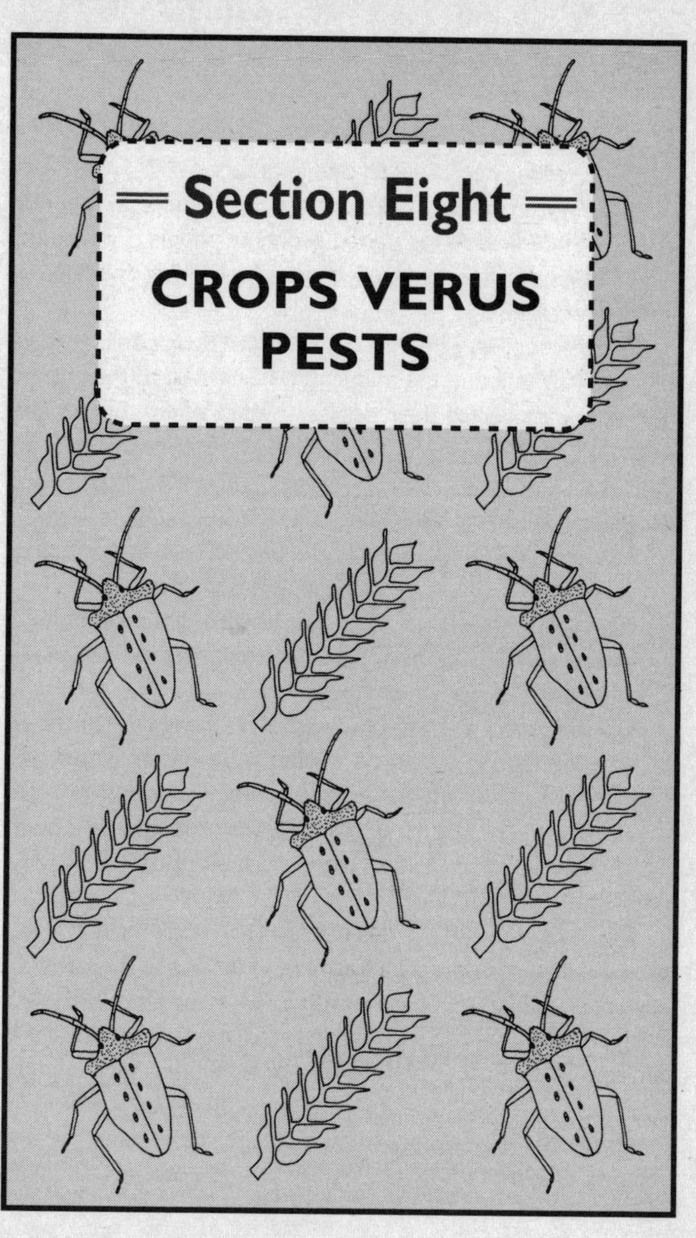
Section Eight
CROPS VERUS PESTS

Since Biblical times, and probably beyond, there have always been people who predict that doomsday is just around the corner.

One of the most famous was Thomas Malthus. In 1798, when the number of people was rising sharply, he warned that population would increase so fast that it would outrun food supplies, leading to mass starvation and disease epidemics.

We've postponed Malthus's predicted day of reckoning for two centuries – thanks mainly to scientific developments in agriculture – but it's beginning to look as though we won't be able to put it off much longer. We're in danger of running out of food.

According to some calculations, Malthus's pessimistic prediction came true in 1989. There were famines before then, of course, but they were local affairs – there wasn't enough food in the places where it was most needed. Ethiopians died in thousands in 1984, while mountains of grain accumulated in Europe. But in 1989 total world food production dipped below the level needed to provide everyone with their minimum nutritional requirements. Famine wasn't a distribution problem any more – now there wasn't enough on the planet to go around.

In 1995 world grain reserves fell to a record low, with just enough in stores to feed the world's population for 48 days. In August 1996 world grain prices soared, as America's grain production plummeted after a devastating combination of droughts and floods wiped out much of the crop.

Meanwhile, the number of people on the planet is rising relentlessly. Today there are nearly six billion souls and by the year 2025 there will be eight and a half billion of us. Some say Earth's human population will rise to around ten billion or more before it begins to level out.

> ***'There is the distinct possibility that we have crossed the threshold where our best efforts may not be enough to retain the food security we have known for most of this century.'***
> ***(Lester Brown, President of the Worldwatch Institute, 1995)***

We could attack the problem by cutting down forests and cultivating more land, as our ancestors have done for the last 10,000 years, but that would mean sacrificing some of Earth's last natural ecosystems, and pushing the species that live in them into extinction.

So a better option may be to use modern technology to boost crop production on existing farms.

It's been done before. In the middle years of the 20th century there was a Green Revolution, when scientists bred crops that could produce massive yield increases if they were supplied with heavy doses of chemical fertilizers. At the same time the chemical industry produced potent pesticides that kept fungi, insects and weeds at bay. For a while it seemed that the food problem had been solved. Countries like India and the Philippines, that had been short of food, now produced more than they needed, and could actually export grain.

There was a price to pay for all this food production. Pollution from crop chemicals became a problem. Wild animals, including some spectacular birds of prey in the United States and Europe, were almost wiped out by pesticide poisoning. Millions of acres of countryside in Europe and North America disappeared under a blanket of intensive agriculture, pushing wildlife to the edge of extinction in some places.

'Agriculture is one of the most powerful technologies on earth. It has the proven potential to cause more environmental havoc than any other human activity.'
(Martha L. Crouch, biotechnologist, 1990)

The first Green Revolution has now run out of steam. If nothing can be done to halt or reverse the trend in population growth, then we need a further change in our ideas. We'll need to produce three times as much food in 2030 as we grow now, to feed the world's population. Genetic engineering might help.

Man versus insects: an arms race

➤One way to boost food production would be to protect it more efficiently from pests. At least 15 per cent of all the food we produce from crop plants is eaten by insects that strip leaves, suck sap, destroy roots and chew their way through stored food. Some insects, like greenfly, damage crops in more subtle ways. They transfer destructive viruses, that stunt plant growth and reduce yields.

Chemical pesticides haven't conquered the insect hordes. They breed in vast numbers and their genes mutate, so they soon become resistant to chemical poisons. Pesticide-resistant mutant insects have emerged and are free to multiply unchecked. But now plant genetic engineers hope that they can bring a new weapon to bear.

☐ Insect multiplication: mind-boggling numbers
A greenfly gives birth to about 20 live young every 20 days. That means that a single, mutant greenfly can leave at least 10,240,000,000,000 descendants in a single growing season.

Round 1: genetic engineers versus pests

➤The gene splicing methods of genetic engineers allow them to add new genes to crops, so that they produce natural chemicals that either kill insect pests or prevent them from feeding on the plants.

These genes can come from all sorts of sources – viruses, bacteria, fungi, animals or even humans. But why should these methods be any better than using chemical sprays?

The case against chemical pesticides

☐ Chemical pesticides are man-made poisons. They often attack insect nervous systems. And if they poison insects, they can sometimes poison us, either when we use them or eat food that has been treated with them.

☐ Many insecticides don't discriminate between insect pests and beneficial insects, like ladybirds. They wipe out friends and foes alike. Once the natural predators of pests have gone, we've no choice but to depend completely on chemical pesticides to protect our crops.

☐ Some chemical pesticides pollute the environment for decades. DDT insecticide has been banned for decades in many countries, but traces of it can still be found in animals and humans that have eaten food contaminated with it. High concentrations of the chemical have recently been found in Italian lakes, many years after the chemical was banned there.

☐ Insect pests quickly become resistant to new chemical pesticides.

☐ Pesticides are expensive, so the poor peasant farmers that need them most can't afford them.

☐ You often have to use chemical pesticides several times during the growth of a crop, when more insects come back. If pesticides are sprayed from the back of a tractor, the tractor damages the crop. They can be sprayed from aircraft, but this is extremely expensive.

The benefits of genetic engineering

☐ The genes that are added to plants are active throughout the whole life of the crop, from the moment its seeds germinate to the time when seeds are harvested. Even the harvested seeds are protected while they're being stored.

☐ Sprays can miss some pests – on the underside of leaves for example – so they multiply and return. Some insect pests feed inside plant stems, where pesticides can't reach them. But every part of a genetically-engineered plant is protected, because the gene defences are in every single cell.

☐ Genes that are added to protect plants from insect attack usually make proteins which upset the insects' digestive system but are harmless to humans. They are safely broken down in our guts, just like any other protein.

☐ Genetically-engineered plants don't kill the harmless predators that help to control pests.

☐ If you grow plants that are genetically engineered to resist pests, you don't need to apply dangerous chemical sprays.

A needle in a haystack

➤Finding suitable genes for protecting crops is slow, difficult and expensive.

The first step in crop plant genetic engineering involves finding genes that might make crops perform better. That's a bit like looking for a needle in a haystack.

If you want to find a gene that's useful in a plant, you first look for its effect. It might make the plant resistant to a fungal disease, for example. Next you try to identify the chemical compound that makes the plant resistant. Then you try to find the gene that makes the compound, cut it out of the chromosome, slot it into a bacterium, and use the bacterium to transfer it into your crop plant. Alternatively, DNA containing the useful genes can be plastered over the surface of microscopic gold particles and fired into plant cells with a particle gun – a technique known as biolistics.

Genetic engineering has great potential benefits to mankind, so some governments have decided to club together and construct complete genetic maps of all the genes in several important organisms, including fruit flies, eelworms, yeast, rice and humans. These maps will show where all the genes can be found. Slowly we'll find out what they do, and the most useful ones can then be put to work in new plants and animals.

In 1996, researchers finally finished mapping and analysing all of the genes in yeast, which is the fungus that is used to brew beer and make bread. It had taken 300 scientists from 100 countries over six years to complete the task.

Yeast only has about 6000 genes, whereas we humans have at least 75,000.

Although scientists now know how many yeast genes exist and understand how they're constructed, they only know what a quarter of them – about 1500 – actually do. It will take several years to find out what the rest are for.

Finding individual genes is a massive task. Finding genes that actually do something useful is even more difficult. The fact that governments are prepared to spend so much money in the quest for useful genes shows just how important they think it is.

'It has been money well spent for Europe's taxpayers.'
(Bruno Hansen, Head of Life Sciences at the European Commission, which helped to pay for the gene mapping in yeast)

The story so far

➤So far, genetic engineers have made some important advances in altering crop plants. They've. . .

- transferred genes that make a protein in snowdrops – which prevents greenfly feeding on their sap – into crop plants. The results are promising. Greenflies feeding on the engineered crops multiply ten times more slowly than on normal plants. The same gene might also protect crops from tiny nematode worms, that eat their roots.

- found a protein in an African plant called a cowpea which protects its seeds from beetles that infest grain stores. The gene for this protein can be transferred to other crops, to protect them from insect attack.
- found a gene in potatoes which can protect rice plants from insects that bore into their stems, where they are out of reach of chemical pesticides.
- found genes in stinging nettles that can protect crops from fungal diseases.

Round 2: revenge of the stem borers

➤There are plenty of promising gene splicing experiments in progress, which could protect crops. But it's too soon to cheer. Some serious problems have reared their ugly heads.

One of the first gene splicing experiments that was designed to beat insect pests used a gene from a bacterium called Bacillus thuringiensis (Bt for short). The gene makes a protein that's poisonous to insects.

Bt is harmless to humans and has been used by farmers and organic gardeners for many years to kill caterpillars. Mix the bacterium with water, spray it on the pests and they shrivel and die in a few days.

The gene responsible for making the poisonous protein inside Bt that makes it lethal to caterpillars has been tracked down and transferred into all sorts of crop plants.

One was maize, which is constantly attacked by a stem boring insect that pesticides can't combat.

Bt worked like a dream to begin with. Healthy maize grew, with the stem borers stopped dead in their tracks.

But then reports began to trickle in from Hawaii and South East Asia that insects were already becoming resistant to the Bt bacterium, even before the genetically-engineered crops were ready to go into production. The insects had rapidly evolved so that they were immune to the Bt that farmers used in the traditional way.

Millions of dollars have been spent in finding Bt's pesticidal protein genes and transferring them into crops. Now it seems that much of this money may have been wasted, if insects have already have found a way around our latest strategy for protecting our crops.

We could soon be back to square one.

Superweeds

➤Many environmental campaigners are not satisfied that enough thought has been given to the safety aspects of crop genetic engineering. There may be hidden environmental hazards.

In 1951 the novelist John Wyndham wrote a chilling science fiction horror story called *The Day of the Triffids*, about a world dominated by giant, stinging plants. Today there are some who say that this science fiction is about to become science fact.

Genespeak
Herbicide – a chemical that kills weeds.

The plant that's provoking all the controversy is herbicide-resistant oilseed rape. Scientists have modified the crop's genes so that oilseed rape can't be killed by certain environmentally safe herbicides that farmers use to zap weeds. This should make weed control easier and more efficient.

In many ways it's a good idea. Weeds reduce crop yields by about ten per cent worldwide. But what would happen if herbicide-resistant crop plants turned into weeds themselves? Could we find ourselves facing new weeds that we couldn't kill with safe herbicides?

Some crop plants, like the yellow-flowered oilseed rape, can already survive as wild plants for short periods. Travel along motorways in spring and you'll see patches of oilseed rape in flower on the verge, growing from seeds that were spilled after harvest on their way to the seed processing plant. It's possible that anything genetic engineers do to improve oilseed rape's survival abilities could turn it into an aggressive weed.

Genespeak
Hybrid – a cross between two species, which inherits some characteristics from each parent. Mules are hybrids between donkeys and horses.

Worse still, what if pollen from the crops was carried on to closely related weeds, so that the crop and weed produced new hybrid strains of herbicide-resistant weeds? We might see the arrival of the 'superweed', immune to chemical herbicides and difficult, expensive and maybe even impossible to control.

So many people are concerned about the safety of introducing herbicide-resistant crops into the countryside. Safety tests show that some of their fears may be justified.

Research has revealed that oilseed rape plants could

easily transfer herbicide resistance to another species of weed that grow beside them. Other experiments have shown that pollen from genetically-engineered oilseed rape can be carried on the wind and pollinate other crops up to two miles away. Once we introduce new genes into a crop that's grown all over the countryside, they might turn up in all sorts of unwelcome places.

Who gains most from herbicide-resistant crops? Some say it's the giant agrochemical companies. They produce the crops and the herbicides that are needed to grow them. One company estimated that the new crops would increase sales of one of their herbicides by $200 million a year.

Vegetable vampires

➤Farming in developing countries can be heartbreaking. Put yourself in the position of a Sudanese farmer who has recently planted a crop of beans.

Everything seems to be going well. The rains come on time. The crop germinates well. You're looking forward to a good harvest.

Then, one morning, while you're walking around the edge of your crop, you notice a strange pink shoot coming up from the roots of one plant. By evening, the shoots are appearing all over the crop, and you know that you and your family are financially ruined.

The shoots belong to a strange parasitic plant called broomrape. Its minute seeds have germinated underground and latched on to the roots of your crop. They've been growing unseen, sucking the life out of the bean plants, until the broomrape flowers are ready to burst through the soil surface. Now the crop is doomed.

When you walk around your crop a few days later, the broomrape flowers are everywhere, and the beans are withering away.

Even if you can afford to buy new seeds, you'll never be able to grow beans on this piece of land again.

Broomrape seeds hang around in the soil for years. A single broomrape bloom can produce 100,000 seeds that are spread by the wind.

Parasitic weeds like broomrape devastate crops in many parts of Africa. About 70 per cent of Nigeria's fields are contaminated with seeds of a parasitic weed called witchweed. In one part of Kenya the same species destroys 81,000 tonnes of maize a year – enough to feed 350,000 people.

Herbicide resistance genes could help. If African crops

were genetically engineered so that they were herbicide resistant, they might be saved from broomrape and witchweed. They could be sprayed with a weed killer that would travel down to their roots without damaging the crop plant. Once the weed killer arrived underground, it would kill the broomrape or witchweed seedlings that were attached to the roots before they could destroy the crop.

It sounds like a good strategy, but its success depends on whether poor Third World farmers can afford to pay for this kind of advanced technology.

> ***'. . . companies pioneering new methods of genetically engineering crops must "reach special agreements" to allow these technologies to be used to help feed people in the poorest parts of the world.'***
> ***(Opinion of Ismail Serageldin, speaking at the UN World Food Summit, November 1996)***

Help yourself

➤Like almost all modern technologies, genetic engineering involves the investment of huge sums of money. Most of this has been spent by multinational companies in the food and agriculture business, who expect to make large profits from genetically-engineered crops.

The biggest profits will come from major crops, like potatoes, wheat, maize and oilseeds that are grown in Europe and North America. Third World farmers depend on a much wider range of tropical crops that we rarely see in the developed world, and the genetic engineering industry isn't so interested in investing research in these, because poor Third World farmers aren't likely to be able to afford to buy expensive, genetically-engineered seeds.

Governments in the Third World quickly realized that they can't rely on the developed world to solve their food production problems. If they wanted to exploit the benefits of genetic engineering, then they would need to do the research themselves. And that's just what's happening in Asia. The work is being done through scientific research funded by international aid agencies.

In one recent example, scientists at the International Rice Research Institute (IRRI) in the Philippines discovered genes that make rice tolerant to floods. Although paddy field rice is grown in soil that's covered with water in the early stages, the crop dies if it's completely submerged.

Sudden floods are common where rice is grown. Monsoon rains create serious flooding and cause an estimated $600 million damage to rice crops every year. The IRRI scientists' discovery means that new varieties can be developed that tolerate flooding for up to two weeks. Farmers will even be able to deliberately flood their crops to kill off weeds which don't have the flooding tolerance gene.

Meanwhile, scientific developments in other parts of the world could soon undermine these agricultural gains in poor countries.

Hidden threats

➤Imagine that you are a farmer in Kenya, growing pyrethrum plants.

Pyrethrum produces a potent natural insecticide, used worldwide, and the crop is valuable. Recently you've been making a good living from your farm. You can afford to send your children to school, build a better house. People in your local community, who work on the farm, are becoming more prosperous.

Things are looking up, but it won't last.

On the other side of the world, in North America, a genetic engineering company has discovered how to put the insecticide genes from pyrethrum into yeast cells. They can grow the yeast in the laboratory and coax it to churn out pyrethrum by the bucketload. Soon, they expect to be able to produce it in their laboratory more cheaply than you Kenyan farmers can.

Now imagine you're the owner of an oil palm plantation in Malaysia.

Most of the local community depend on your plantation for work. But their world could soon fall apart, thanks to genetic engineering inventions in North America.

There, genetic engineers have found a way to persuade oilseed rape crops to produce palm oil. If things go well – and they're looking good – then American farmers will soon be producing their own palm oil for use in soaps, detergents, bath oils and cosmetics. No need to import the oil from Malaysia any more.

Technologies like these, where scientists are altering crops to produce products that developed countries normally import from the Third World, are going on all over Europe and North America. It doesn't take much imagination to guess what effect it will have on the poor farmers of the Third World. If they can't earn foreign currency by exporting their crop products, they have no money to invest in schools, hospitals and all the other things that their local communities need.

Genetically-engineered crops are a ticking high-technology time-bomb that could disrupt world trade in plant products. The outlook could be bleak for poor tropical countries that export plant raw materials if we can genetically engineer an alternative, home-grown supply.

> ***'Unlike almost any other technology, it [agricultural technology] can provide cheap products for the very poor. But equally it can be captured by the rich, and that is what is in danger of happening.'***
> ***(Gordon Conway, author of a major report for the Consultative Group on International Agricultural Research on the future of agricultural research, 1996)***

Section Nine
PLASTIC PLANTS

It's hard to imagine life without plastics, but they're a relatively recent invention. Plastics only became common in everyday objects in the second half of the 20th century.

Plastics are an essential part of modern life, but they have their drawbacks. One problem is that they're produced from oil and that will eventually run out. Another is that their production involves a great deal of pollution, ranging from oil spills from tankers to the toxic wastes and polluting gases that are produced from plastics factories.

One of the benefits of plastics is that many are tough and almost indestructible, but this creates another set of problems when they're thrown away. They can pollute the environment for centuries, without breaking down. Walk along any beach and you're sure to find plastic objects that have been washed ashore after months or years of floating in the sea.

So imagine a plastic that's made in plants, using free energy from sunlight, rain that falls from the clouds, minerals in the soil and carbon dioxide in the air. Better still, imagine a plastic that breaks down when you've finished with it into water and carbon dioxide, leaving no traces; a plastic that's completely biodegradable, that you can throw on a compost heap, where it will rapidly disappear.

Genetic engineers are well on the way to mass producing this magical material.

Genespeak
Biodegradable – material that decays when it's attacked by natural organisms like bacteria and fungi.

It already exists naturally in a bacterium, which makes tiny granules of a plastic called polyhydroxybutyrate – or PHB for short. But PHB is expensive to produce. You have to grow the bacteria that make it in a warm broth in massive vats in a factory, and feed them with expensive energy sources.

But now scientists are transferring the genes for PHB production from bacteria into plants. Farmers could soon be growing crops of plastic.

Plants like this, that produce raw materials instead of food products are called industrial crops. We can expect to see many more of them in the countryside in the future.

Some diesel buses already run on vegetable oils extracted from plants, instead of mineral oil pumped out of the ground.

But the possibilities for using genetic engineering to persuade plants to produce new products doesn't end there. One day we may find ourselves eating plants that contain medicines.

An apple a day

➤There is an old saying that 'an apple a day keeps the doctor away'. We might need to rephrase that soon, to 'an apple a day keeps the dentist away', because scientists have discovered a way of preventing tooth decay by modifying the food that we eat.

Genespeak
Antibodies – molecules in the body that attack and destroy organisms that cause diseases.

Human blood contains complicated compounds called antibodies, that grab disease organisms and destroy them.

Recently, antibodies have been discovered that attack bacteria that cause tooth decay. These useful molecules can protect teeth from decay for months – even if you don't clean your teeth.

At the moment the antibodies have to be painted on teeth. In the future they could be put into plants that we eat. Genetic engineers could transfer the antibody genes from people into plant products like apples, so that every time you ate a fruit the antibodies in it would destroy any tooth decay bacteria in your mouth.

It's an intriguing possibility, but we're probably not ready for it just yet. This is because plants like this would be very difficult to classify. Are they foods? Or are they drugs, being used in a medical treatment?

There are extremely strict safety regulations controlling the testing and use of new drugs, which might make the development of all-in-one food and medicines far too expensive. The costs of safety testing of a new drug can easily exceed £20 million. If food plants with genetically engineered medicines inside have to be tested in the same way, they might not prove to be so attractive.

In some ways this could be a pity, because adding genes to fresh foods to protect us from disease could solve some serious health problems.

Scientists are currently trying to add genes to bananas which will immunize people against food poisoning. Many other drugs could be delivered in the same way, as part of our everyday diet.

Bloodsuckers

➤Doctors have used leeches to remove blood from patients since the days of the ancient Greeks, who believed that too much blood was a cause of illness.

Today the practice has almost vanished, but medicine still has a use for leeches.

These blood-sucking worms produce a chemical compound called hirudin, which they inject into wounds as soon as their fangs penetrate their host's flesh. Hirudin stops blood clotting, ensuring that the leech's blood meal flows uninterrupted.

Hirudin is a useful compound in medicine because it can stop potentially fatal blood clots from forming in the arteries of hospital patients. It's still prepared from medicinal leeches, but these animals are now rare. So genetic engineers have come up with an alternative strategy for producing this life-saving material. They've succeeded in transferring the hirudin gene to plants, which might now make hirudin in large quantities.

Hirudin is just one of many medicinal compounds that could be made in crops that are currently only used as a source of food. In the long term this kind of strategy could also prove to be one of the best ways of exploiting valuable medicinal compounds that are found in tropical rain forests.

Save the rainforest

> ***Genespeak***
> ***Pharmacy – a place were medicines are prepared and distributed.***

➤One of the best reasons for saving tropical rain forests is that the plants that grow there contain all sorts of useful natural medicines that can heal the sick and save lives. The tribes that live in the forest have used the plants around them as a natural pharmacy for thousands of years.

So it's not surprising that international drugs companies are keen to exploit this wonderful natural source of medicines. But once they've found them, how should they produce them?

One possibility would be to cut down the trees and extract their natural chemicals, but this would destroy the forest.

Another way would be to cultivate the rain forest plants as a crop, but this would mean destroying more of the natural environment, to create agricultural land for growing the crops in plantations. And it takes a long time to develop wild plants into high-yielding crops. It's taken humans 10,000 years to convert wheat from a scruffy weed into the productive crop that it is today.

A much better alternative might be to find the genes that produce the drugs. Then we could use genetic engineering techniques to transfer these to crops that we can already grow well, like oilseed rape, wheat and maize. That way, we could exploit rain forest genes without destroying the forest itself.

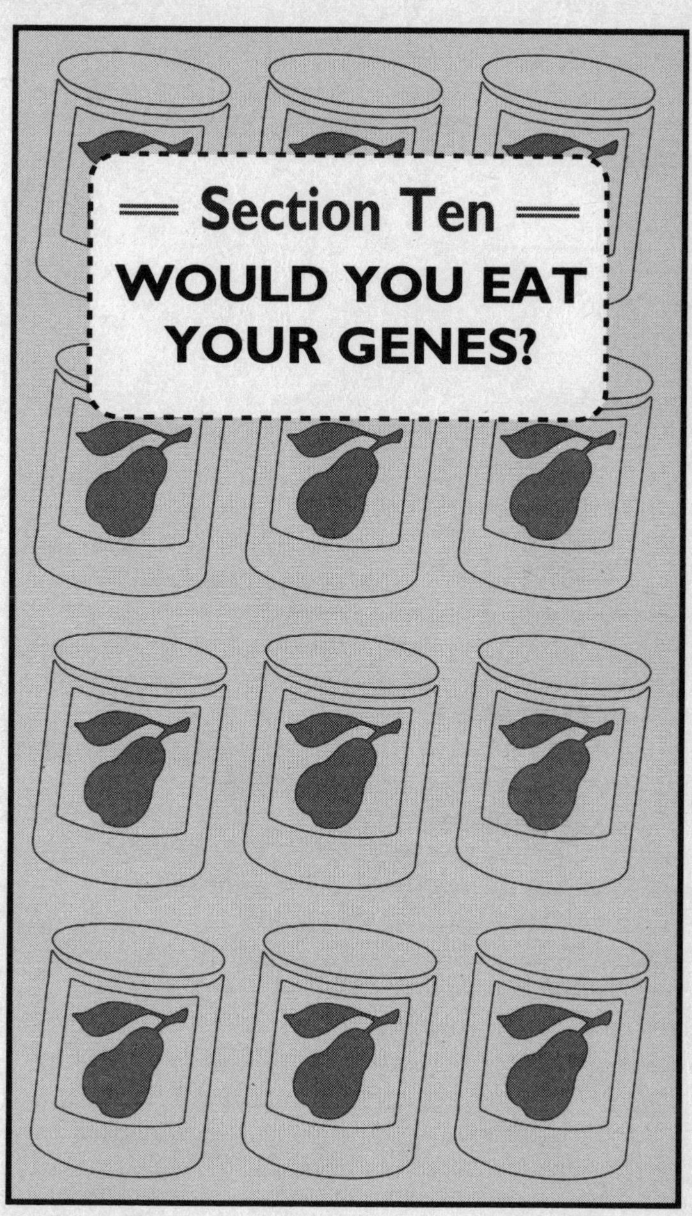
Section Ten
WOULD YOU EAT YOUR GENES?

Genetic engineers have already produced crops like the Flavr Savr tomato, which can be bought in supermarkets in the United States. One of its ripening genes has been knocked out, making it less likely to be damaged during transport and ensuring that it lasts longer on the supermarket shelf, before it begins to rot.

Long-life tomatoes might not seem to be the most exciting way to use our new-found knowledge of the DNA molecule, but other developments in genetically modified foods could bring major health benefits. For example, proteins that are important in our diets could be added to foods where they are not normally found.

This could be a real bonus, but there might be hazards too, as one American genetic engineering company found when they transferred genes from Brazil nuts to soya beans. The plan was that the genes would make the proteins in the beans more nutritious. The reality was that some people are allergic to Brazil nuts. Most of them became ill when they ate the genetically-engineered soy bean protein. After that, the project was abandoned.

Genetic engineers say they can give us better crops that can be grown with fewer chemicals, produce more nutritious food and can be processed more easily.

But there are many more possibilities to explore. Genes have been discovered that alter the quality of fats in our diet, so that they reduce the risk of heart disease. Fats make up 30 per cent of the energy supply in our food, but some fats block arteries with deposits of cholesterol, which interrupts the blood supply and causes heart attacks.

Researchers in Texas have found genes in a plant called borage that produce gamma linolenic acid, a chemical compound that reduces the risk of heart attacks caused by cholesterol. Now they have transferred the gene into crops that produce the oils that are used to make margarine and ice-cream. This should make these fatty foods healthier and safer.

In other projects, genetic engineers have equipped potatoes with a gene from bacteria which cuts down the sugar level in potato tubers, so that they make better potato crisps. Genes have also been found that will reduce the amount of caffeine in coffee, making it safer to drink in large amounts.

Unnatural Science

➤Many people are wary of genetically-engineered foods and refuse to buy them, for all sorts of reasons.

One objection is that it's unnatural to move genes around in this way. Scientists are doing something that can't happen in nature. They're behaving like gods, creating new life forms. Genes from animals, for example, never move into plants naturally, so we should leave them where they belong.

If you eat a cabbage that's got a human gene in it, does that make you a cannibal?

Many people have strong religious objections to this kind of science. They consider that it's wrong for man to meddle with God's creations in this way.

'Say no to blackened catfish with trout hormone and cornbread with firefly gene.' (Car sticker in the US)

If the objectors really believe that genetic manipulation of food is unnatural, and should be banned, then genetic engineers wonder why they didn't raise the issue sooner. Scientists who breed crops without using genetic engineering have been doing unnatural things to plants for most of this century.

They've put barley genes into wheat, to make it disease resistant, by forcing the two species to cross in the laboratory without the aid of any of the modern genetic engineering techniques. No one batted an eyelid when this 'unnatural' wheat was used to make bread.

A whole new crop species – called triticale – has been created by crossing wheat and rye. No one raised any objections. So some scientists argue that genetic engineers are merely pushing science a little further forward.

They argue that genetic engineering is just the exploitation and extension of a natural process. Even the bacterium that they use to shuttle genes between organisms is common in the soil. It's probably been infecting plants and transferring genes between species for millions of years.

Recently it's been discovered that some micro-organisms may have been moving genes between animals naturally for millions of years too. A gene from a fruit fly was found in a human chromosome. It turned up in people who suffer from a rare disease called Charcot-Marie-Tooth disease, which destroys the muscles of the legs and feet. Scientists call the gene 'mariner', because it travels around constantly like a mariner on the oceans. It's a peculiar type of gene, called a jumping gene, that can cut itself out of chromosomes and paste itself into new locations, causing genetic defects along the way. It probably travelled from fruit flies to humans inside a virus.

So switching genes between organisms that are as different as insects and mammals might not be as unnatural as it sounds. All we're doing, say some scientists, is using natural processes for the good of mankind.

But consumer groups are not convinced. They want to be able to choose between 'natural' foods and those that have been genetically engineered.

A large number of chefs in Germany and the United States have joined in campaigns to boycott all genetically-engineered foods. They've given them a new name: 'Frankenfoods.'

Your right to choose

➤Perhaps the best policy would be to let the customers choose, but they can only do that if the products of the new technologies are labelled. That's something that the genetic engineering industry isn't keen on.

They say that the very words 'genetic engineering' frighten people, because of a bad image created in the press. If these words appear on labels, people won't buy their products even if they're perfectly safe.

'If they refuse to provide information about what goes into our food, or how they produced it, you can't help wondering whether they have something to hide.' (Supermarket shopper)

And there's a practical problem with labelling everything. There just wouldn't be room on labels to provide a full explanation of the production of all genetically-engineered ingredients in – say – a can of soup.

Calgene, the company that produced the Flavr Savr tomato, got around this problem by supplying an explanatory leaflet that sits on the shelf next to the product. But this isn't really a long-term solution. If leaflets have to be produced for every new genetically-engineered food, supermarket shelves would soon be submerged in a sea of paper with information that busy shoppers wouldn't have time to read. A trip to do the weekend shopping could end up like a visit to a library.

Food labelling is far from complete now. Most people have little idea what's in their food or how it's produced. Until recently, few people realized that the gelatine in jellies and jelly babies is made from boiled cattle bones. This was only publicized in 1996, when it was discovered that some of the cattle might have been infected with BSE, which can cause Creutzfeldt-Jacob disease and destroy the human brain.

Jews and Muslims are concerned about food which might contain genes from pigs and other animals which their religious laws forbid them to eat.

It does seem that most people would be happier if they knew more about the contents of their food, and how it was made.

Vegetarians are particularly anxious to know whether animal genes might be transferred into the plant products that they eat.

At the moment it looks as though governments might make genetic engineering companies label genetically-engineered foods which are fresh, where the cells are still alive. The reason for this is that live cells contain intact DNA, with genes that might be transferred from the plant DNA into bacteria that live in the human gut. There is a real but remote possibility that this could happen. This labelling rule would apply to things like fruit, vegetables and eggs.

But food manufacturers wouldn't be forced to label cooked foods, where the cells are dead and the DNA they contain has been destroyed by heating.

GREENPEACE BLOCKADES BEANS WITH NEW GENES
(Newspaper headline, The Independent, Saturday 30 November 1996)

Some supermarket chains, who are worried about consumers' suspicion of genetically-engineered products, have offered to label these foods voluntarily, but one major producer of genetically-engineered soy beans has already undermined their plans.

In 1996, a cargo of genetically-engineered, herbicide-resistant soy beans was imported into Britain, despite the attempts of protestors to blockade the ships that carried it. The genetically-engineered seeds had been mixed with normal seeds, so they couldn't be identified and rejected by food processing companies. They'll end up in thousands of different food products on supermarket shelves. Supermarkets won't be able to label genetically-engineered foods, because most will have genetically-engineered soy bean as an ingredient.

In a recent poll 93 per cent of UK consumers said that they wanted genetically-engineered products to be labelled; the mixed soy bean imports have made that impossible.

Even if you wanted to choose, you can't!

'. . . foisting genetically-engineered foods on the market without labelling is not exactly a recipe for building public confidence.'
(Julie Sheppard, The Genetics Forum, 1996)

Section Eleven
A MONSTER OUT OF CONTROL

The Frankenstein Factor

➤In the 1980s scientists at Beltsville in Maryland, USA, carried out a genetic engineering experiment whose gruesome results have haunted science ever since.

They tried to make pigs grow faster by giving them human genes that produce one of the hormones that controls our growth. Sure enough, the pigs grew faster, but they were hideously deformed. They developed chronic arthritis and several other defects that ensured that experiments like this would be the target of violent objections by animal rights activists everywhere.

The popular press had already raised the spectre of scientists creating Frankenstein-like monsters, so the Beltsville experiment seemed to confirm people's worst fears about the antics of genetic engineers.

The real problem with this is that talk of creating monsters often hides some of the more subtle, but far more dangerous risks, of creating genetically-engineered animals.

Genespeak
Transgenic – an organism that has been modified by genetic engineers, by transferring a gene into it from another animal, plant or micro-organism.

Super salmon

➤Take, for example, the case of the transgenic salmon. Salmon are often raised in underwater cages, in fish farms. The faster they grow, the more money the salmon farmers make, so scientists have experimented with equipping salmon with genes for hormones that will make them grow faster – ten times faster. They don't necessarily become giants, but they mature more quickly, in two years instead of three, so they can be sold sooner.

The trouble is that some farmed fish always escape. There are already five times as many fish farm salmon as wild salmon in some Norwegian fjords. And no one really knows what effect genetically-engineered super-fish would have on wild fish populations. Will they compete better for food supplies and wipe out their wild ancestors? Will the bigger males that escaped from fish farms displace wild males, so they pass on their genes to wild populations?

Fortunately, with the super-salmon there is a solution to one of these problems: the genetic engineers can make the fish sterile, so they can't interbreed with wild fish.

But breeding 'super salmon' is just one of many genetic engineering experiments being carried out on fish that could have far-reaching effects on wild species. Carp with extra growth hormone genes that make them grow many times their normal size have been bred. These have voracious appetites and grow much faster than wild fish. They could create havoc in natural ecosystems.

Anti-freeze genes, that prevent the blood of Arctic and Antarctic fish from turning to ice, have been transferred to other edible species. This will allow the transgenic fish to thrive in colder waters. What will it do to the balance of natural ecosystems? No one knows. Time will tell.

Scientists expect to be able to produce chickens that lay eggs constantly, by removing the gene for the hormone that makes them become broody and stop laying. Egg production could be boosted by 20 per cent.

Crying over spilt milk

➤One of the most controversial uses of genetic engineering in food production so far has been the development of a growth hormone that makes cattle produce more milk.

The growth hormone is called bovine somatotropin – or BST for short. It's made by genetically-engineered bacteria in the laboratory. The BST has been transferred from cattle to the bacterium, which then makes large amounts of the hormone. Once this has been extracted and purified, it can be supplied to cattle. This extra dose of hormone means that they produce up to ten per cent more milk than untreated cows.

This is one of the first products of the genetic engineering industry to be used in agriculture on animals. It's said to have cost more than a billion dollars to develop and it's become a test case for public opinion on the use of genetic engineering technology in agriculture. A war of words has been waged over BST ever since. The arguments went something like this. . .

It'll cut costs and make milk cheaper:

The companies produced the hormone originally to boost milk yields and make dairy farming more profitable. If farmers used BST they could produce more milk from fewer cows, cutting production costs.

It's unfair to small farmers:

Only wealthy, successful farmers can afford this new technology. They'll be able to cut costs and produce cheaper milk, and this will drive poorer farmers out of business. In the end, BST could cause unemployment and hardship in small farming communities.

It's cruel to cows:

Trials went ahead anyway. The product worked well.

But it was soon claimed that cows that produce so much milk can suffer from severe inflammation of their udders and develop an infection called mastitis. Mastitis produces pus in milk, which was detected at higher levels in cows that had been treated with BST. Forcing cows to produce so much milk was downright cruel, claimed animal welfare activists.

It's a health hazard for humans:

There were also fears that BST might find its way into milk and cause health problems for people who drank it. No one was sure what a dose of BST would do to human growth, but opponents saw this as a real risk. The companies assured them it was safe.

OK. You can use the hormone, but label milk so we can choose not to buy it:

A campaign grew to ban the use of the compound, but by now milk from BST-treated cows was on sale in American supermarkets. Some supermarkets decided to label the product from the treated cows, so that consumers who objected to its use could choose to leave it on the shelf.

Do that and we'll sue you:

In retaliation the companies that produced the drug, and stood to lose millions of dollars if farmers didn't use it, threatened to sue supermarkets who labelled their products. They claimed that there was absolutely no difference between milk produced from BST-treated cows and milk from cows that hadn't received the injections.

Keep your BST. We've already got too much milk in Europe:

Meanwhile, the American biotechnology companies tried to market BST in Europe. European countries produce far too much milk and farmers already face restrictions on milk production. Why, asked the politicians, should we authorize a treatment that makes cattle produce even more milk, when our taxpayers are already subsidizing farmers to produce less? And in Europe, just as in the United States, the same arguments raged about mastitis, human health and the effect of introducing the drug on the livelihoods of smaller farmers. Claims that the companies that were producing BST had suppressed reports about the effects of the drug on animal health fanned the flames of controversy.

Use BST, or we'll start a trade war:

So far, the widespread use of BST hasn't been authorized in Europe, and the companies that produce it are becoming increasingly frustrated. They threaten retaliation against European biotechnology companies that try to market their products in the US.

. . . and so the row rumbles on. What started as a simple scientific invention to boost milk yields has grown into an international economic confrontation over cruelty to animals, unfair competition, unemployment, human health and the right of consumers to know how their food has been produced.

And, perhaps most importantly, it has forced people to ask how far we should use our knowledge of genetics to exploit animals.

Animal rights

➤There are rumours of experiments that show that it's possible to put growth hormone genes in chickens that will make them grow heavier faster. The trouble is that their legs are too weak to bear the extra weight, so they break under the strain.

Just how far can we go in our exploitation of animals? Are genetic engineers treating farm animals, which can feel pain and distress, like machines designed for the production of food? Once again, there are strong views on both sides of the argument. . .

> ***'. . . this is the front-line battle for animal rights across the world for the next 50 years.' Jeremy Rifkin, American Environmentalist.***

Genetic engineering techniques make animals that we eat larger, leaner or faster growing. People have used ordinary selective breeding techniques to do this since animals were first domesticated. The objectives haven't changed – we're just using a technique that does the same things more efficiently.

But it isn't the same. The old, selective breeding techniques didn't allow you to put human genes in pigs. Genetic engineering lets you switch genes between species that never interbreed in nature.

At least we don't set out to produce deformities in animals. People who breed pet animals, like many modern dog breeds, produce mutants that suffer from severe disabilities and weaknesses because they've been bred for peculiar characteristics to please the fancy of their owners. It's hypocritical to turn a blind eye to the breeding of deformed mutant animals by traditional means for pets, and criticize us for developing better techniques for producing more efficient animals for feeding hungry people.

But genetic engineering has gone further than just producing more efficient farm animals for food. It's turning them into four-legged drug factories.

Farmaceuticals

➤Farm animals are indeed being genetically modified to produce drugs, founding a new industry which is often called farmaceuticals.

Some drugs are already made in the laboratory by cultures of genetically-engineered cells, like yeast for example. But soon they could be made in much larger quantities by farm animals.

A few unfortunate people lack key molecules in their bodies that they need for survival. One example is the genetic disease called haemophilia, where victims cannot make the protein that causes their blood to clot. If they cut themselves, they can bleed to death.

One way to make these essential molecules is to equip farm animals like sheep and goats with the missing human genes. Then the animals secrete the proteins into their milk and the proteins can be extracted and used to treat patients suffering from diseases.

Experiments like these are the basis of a rapidly expanding industry. In future, many essential medical molecules will be produced in flocks of sheep that carry a few human genes in their chromosomes.

In fact, all sorts of animals could be used for the production of useful molecules. The new industry plans to exploit animals ranging from caterpillars (for raising large amounts of genetically-engineered viruses that can be used in pest control programmes), to sheep (that produce life-saving drugs in their milk).

The new technology is forcing us to rethink our relationship with animals. Do we have the right to redesign them for our own purposes?

Grace, a genetically engineered goat, produces an anti-cancer drug in her milk.

Tracey is a sheep who has been modified to produce a protein called human alpha-1-antitrypsin in her milk. This can be used to treat children suffering from cystic fibrosis.

Hermann, a genetically-engineered bull born in 1990,

carries a gene for lactoferrin, another medicinally important product.

Doomed mice

Genespeak
Oncology – the study of cancers

➤Until now, it's mice that have born the brunt of most of the genetic engineering experiments. Laboratory mice have been used for decades in medical and genetic research, but now they've become a test case in the controversy over animal rights. Three experiments in particular have caused public alarm.

One is the oncomouse, produced at Harvard University as an experimental animal for cancer research. Oncomice have been given a gene that means that they always develop cancerous tumours once they reach a certain age. All oncomice are doomed to die of the disease unless anti-cancer treatments can be found to save them. They might help scientists to discover cures for cancers in humans.

Another is the hairless mouse, bred by a drugs company that wanted to use it to test chemicals that might act as hair restorers for bald men.

And then there's the mouse whose genes have been altered so that human tissues will grow on its body. It could be used for growing human skin, that could then be grafted on to people who need skin grafts. One of these mice has been used to grow a full-sized human ear in the middle of its back.

Is it immoral to genetically engineer animals in this way, even if they offer hope for finding new ways of saving human life?

Patent office officials clearly thought so, when they refused to grant a patent on the hairless mouse, on the grounds that it was 'immoral' because its use involved suffering to the animal that outweighed the benefits to people.

The question we all have to answer is whether we value human life above all other animal life.

If you believe that animals can be subjected to any treatment if a human life might be saved, then the answer is easy: the breeding of the oncomouse is justified.

If you don't, then the questions are much more difficult, because you have to ask how much suffering we can inflict on animals in the interests of human health and happiness.

Could you vote against a ban on genetic engineering experiments with mice, even if they might one day produce a cure for a disease that might kill you, or kill someone you loved? Would you vote for a ban on techniques and deny other people the possibility of cures for their illnesses?

There's another factor to consider too: money. The inventors of the oncomouse and hairless mouse wanted to patent them, so that any researchers who want to use them in cancer research would have to pay fees to the oncomouse owners. This raises another difficult question: is it immoral for the people who genetically engineered the suffering mice to make financial profits from their work?

When courts in the United States debated this question they didn't seem to think so, because they quickly granted a patent to the discoverers of the oncomouse. In Europe the courts weren't so sure and the patent application was refused several times.

Issues like this can divide society right down the middle.

Eco terrorists

➤What can people do if they don't agree with the way in which genetic engineering is being used?

Most protestors lend their support to organizations like Greenpeace, Compassion in World Farming or The Genetics Forum. They also write letters of protest to politicians and to companies that are involved in developing or selling genetically-engineered products. This is the proper, democratic way to bring about change.

But in extreme cases there have been people who have taken direct action, because they are violently opposed to the use of genetic engineering.

In Europe a group who call themselves the Fiery Viruses have wrecked scores of plant genetic engineering experiments in France, the Netherlands and Switzerland, because they're worried about potential risks to the environment. Similar groups have targeted laboratories where genetic-engineering experiments are carried out on animals.

Earth First! – a radical environmental group – destroyed potato plants at a research station in California that were about to be sprayed with a genetically-engineered bacterium that prevents frost damage.

The genetic engineering industry sees these people as eco-terrorists, but their actions show that there is a deep-rooted opposition to the new technology in some sections of society. Biotechnology has raised new concerns over human health, invasive plants and our relationship with the animals that we domesticate.

But the issue that creates real dread involves organisms that we can't even see.

Section Twelve
PANDORA'S BOX

Prometheus stole fire from the sun and gave it to humans to use, against the wishes of Jupiter. Jupiter planned his revenge.

He would give Prometheus a booby-trapped wife. He persuaded Vulcan to make her from clay and bring her to life, then asked other gods to make her irresistible. By the time they'd finished she had beauty, grace, eloquence, a beautiful singing voice and rich jewels.

Jupiter himself donated the final gift – a beautiful box which she had to give to her future husband as a marriage present – and then named her Pandora, which means 'someone who has every necessary gift'.

Prometheus smelled a rat and rejected Pandora before she could captivate him with her charms. So she married his brother Epimetheus instead, who accepted Pandora's box and opened it. As he lifted the lid every evil, pestilence and disease that has brought human misery from that day to this flew out.

In revenge for Prometheus's theft of fire, the gods punished humans by releasing plagues that deliver death and disease.

A modern nightmare

Genespeak
Micro-organisms – minute, single-celled forms of life, like bacteria and viruses.

➤The moral of this story is that you can get your fingers badly burned if you play with fire.

There are many people who fear that genetic engineers play with fire when they meddle with bacteria, viruses and other microscopic agents of disease. They're opening Pandora's box again, say the critics.

If we use modern genetic techniques to alter plants, animals or even ourselves, we can remain in control of our creations. They are relatively easy to see, find and destroy if they become a threat.

Micro-organisms are different. We can't see them, but they're everywhere. Once we let loose a new, genetically-engineered version of a virus that can survive in the wild, it can never be put back into its test tube. And accidents with micro-organisms do happen. . .

Doomsday for rabbits

➤White settlers took rabbits to Australia. Now the continent is covered with millions of these fast-breeding pests that destroy A$600 million (£315 million)-worth of crops every year. Past attempts to wipe them out with the myxomatosis virus have failed because the rabbits have become resistant to this disease. But now microbiologists have come up with something better.

It's called calicivirus, and it's lethal.

But before it could be let loose on rabbits, calicivirus had to be tested. Scientists had to be sure that it wouldn't kill koalas and other native Australian mammals. So they took it to Wardang Island, off the coast of South Australia, and let it go. It spread like wildfire, wiping out rabbits with frightening efficiency.

But then, in October 1995, the unthinkable happened. Somehow – perhaps carried in the wind – the virus reached the mainland long before safety tests were completed. By April 1996 it had spread to every state in Australia. Calicivirus crossed the continent faster than anyone had believed possible, leaving millions of dead rabbits in its wake. Scientists still aren't certain that it can't kill koalas, kangaroos, wombats and other elements of Australia's unique wildlife. Now all they can do is keep their fingers crossed.

So it's hardly surprising that people are fearful of what will happen when scientists release new forms of micro-organisms.

There was a public outcry in 1993, when researchers from Oxford University added scorpion toxin genes to viruses that kill caterpillars and let them loose on cabbage pests in a field next to a small Oxfordshire village. What if the virus wiped out caterpillars of moths that weren't pests? What if it mutated, and began to attack the larvae of harmless butterflies? Concern has never died down, even though the researchers used a special technique to disable the virus, so that it couldn't survive in the environment for long.

Are scientists playing roulette with the future of our wildlife?

Risky business

➤With so much at stake, why do genetic engineers meddle with micro-organisms?

The reason is that fungi, bacteria and viruses are extremely versatile organisms whose benefits far outweigh the damage they do. It's true that they cause dreaded diseases like HIV, Ebola, bubonic plague and tuberculosis, and also destroy our crops and domestic animals. But for each of these enemies there are many more micro-organisms that are beneficial.

In the environment they break down dead organisms and recycle their nutrients. They increase soil fertility by turning atmospheric nitrogen gas into nitrate fertilizer.

They are part of the natural ecosystem, regulating the numbers of pests.

If it wasn't for micro-organisms the land would be covered in a deep layer of dead, undecayed vegetation, and the soil would be starved of nutrients.

We use micro-organisms in food production, for making beer, bread and wine, and for making medicines. The skills of scientists in modifying viruses and bacteria in the past have allowed them to invent treatments like vaccination, which protects us from some of the worst occupants of Pandora's Box.

Deep-sea developments

Genespeak
Extremophiles – micro-organisms that can live at extremely high or low temperatures, or in extremely acid or alkaline conditions that will kill most forms of life.

➤Bacteria are the oldest living organisms on Earth and are very similar to some of the first living things that evolved. They've been here for three and a half billion years in more or less the same form. They are the most successful organisms on Earth, in terms of ability to survive and in terms of sheer numbers.

Nothing comes near bacterial cells' versatility when it comes to living in difficult situations. They can survive in boiling water and freezing Arctic conditions. Some thrive in salty, alkaline and acid conditions.

In Japan scientists are trying to isolate genes from a deep-sea bacteria called Pyrococcus shinkai, which lives around hot thermal vents at enormous pressures, thousands of feet below the surface. Its cells contain proteins and enzymes that work at high temperatures that would destroy lesser organisms. The genes that make these molecules could be spliced into bacteria that we already use in industrial processes, making them more versatile.

There are scores of projects around the world that aim to modify micro-organisms in beneficial ways. In every case, scientists need to weigh up the costs and benefits, and try to predict what might go wrong. They have to calculate the risks of the worst imaginable accidents.

Tempting target1: free nitrogen fertilizer

➤A microscopic bacterium called Rhizobium leguminosarum lives in nodules on the roots of bean plants. It turns nitrogen from the air into nitrate fertilizer that beans can use for growth. If we could genetically engineer grass roots so that they would form these nodules, then we might. . .

Pro

☐ grow pastures and crops like wheat that wouldn't need nitrogen fertilizers: they'd get it from nitrogen in the air, thanks to the bacteria;

☐ make food production cheaper;

☐ reduce water pollution, because much of the nitrogen fertilizer that we add to crops ends up in the water supply, damaging wildlife habitats and human health;

☐ reduce industrial pollution, because production of nitrogen fertilizers uses a lot of energy and creates pollution.

Con

☐ release a bacterium that might mutate and attach itself to roots of wild grasses, upsetting the balance of natural ecosystems. These rampant, self-fertilising grasses might smother rare wild plants.

Plans to market one new, genetically-engineered variety of Rhizobium were halted in 1995, while more tests were carried out to find out if it might invade natural ecosystems.

Tempting target 2: immunizing plants

➤If small, harmless parts of viruses are spliced into the cells of crop plants, they become immune to serious virus attacks. If we used this technique we might. . .

Pro

☐ ***protect crops from viruses that cause billions of pounds worth of damage every year, and boost food production.***

Con

☐ ***run the risk of creating new virus diseases. Tests have shown that disease viruses can modify themselves with the bits of virus that are engineered into the crop plant cells. We might create an even worse virus problem.***

Better safe than sorry

➤With so much at stake, the rules for releasing genetically-engineered micro-organisms are usually much stricter than rules for dealing with larger plants and animals. And it's reassuring to know that there are already some examples of cautious scientists putting a brake on projects that might be too risky, as one recent example in Australia demonstrates.

Some wild plants in the Australian outback contain a deadly compound called fluoracetate. It acts like cyanide and poisons cattle and sheep. Fluoracetate has evolved naturally, to stop grazing animals making a meal of plants. Sadly, domestic animals seem to be slow learners and every year thousands die when they eat the poisonous foliage.

In one incident 17,000 sheep from a flock of 70,000 were killed. This kind of poisoning costs the average Australian stock farmer A$140,000 per year (£67,000).

Genetic engineers have modified a bacterium called Butyrvibrio fibrisolvens that lives in sheep and cattle guts, so that it protects the animals by breaking down lethal fluoracetate before it can kill them.

It's easy to use. Inoculate one cow with the modified bacterium and this animal will then spread it to every other cow in the herd, when their mouths touch. Butyrvibrio could wipe out deaths from fluoracetate poisoning, but there's a problem that wasn't foreseen when the research started.

What if the bacterium spreads into the gut of wild grazing animals, like kangaroos? Many of the plants that live in the Australian outback only survive because they're protected from grazers by their fluoracetate. If wild grazers could eat them, the plants would become extinct, the sparse vegetation would disappear and the area might become a barren desert.

So, for now at least, the use of this genetically modified bacterium has been banned. It needs more work, to make sure that it's safe.

The nightmare scenario

➤When genetic engineers transfer genes between organisms, they have to be sure that their experiments have worked. Often there's no way of knowing that a gene has been successfully inserted in a group of cells, if it doesn't do anything that you can actually see with the naked eye.

How can you tell that the tiny plant you're growing from a single, genetically-engineered cell really contains an insect resistance gene? It might be months before it's large enough to test by exposing it to pests.

You need another gene that does something that you can easily see. If you add this to your engineered plant alongside the gene you're really interested in, it will tell you whether both genes have really been transferred to their new host.

Genetic engineers call these genes reporter genes, because they report back instantly if their experiments have worked. One way of doing this is to add genes for antibiotic resistance alongside the experimental gene.

Antibiotics are chemicals that kill living cells. Any genetically-engineered cells that contain a gene for antibiotic resistance will survive if they are treated with antibiotics, letting the scientist know that his gene transfer experiment has worked.

Antibiotics are one of the greatest medical advances of the 20th century, because they're so effective at wiping out some of the bacterial infections that have killed millions of people in the past. Penicillin is the most famous example, discovered by Nobel prize winner Sir Alexander Fleming in 1928.

Unfortunately, bacteria are very adaptable organisms. Threaten them with a chemical that might wipe them all out and they'll mutate, so that some become resistant to it.

And that's what has been happening ever since antibiotics were first discovered. Just when it seems as though a bacterial disease has been defeated, a new strain mutates that's resistant to antibiotics. Then the disease flares up again.

The situation is becoming critical, because far too many antibiotics have been prescribed, often unnecessarily. So the overuse of antibiotics has encouraged the rapid evolution of new antibiotic-resistant mutants almost everywhere.

We thought that we had defeated tuberculosis, which killed thousands in past centuries. But in 1995 three million people worldwide died from the disease – more than in any year in history. In many cases people were infected with an antibiotic-resistant form of the tuberculosis bacterium.

So today doctors have their backs to the wall. They're now using antibiotics which they describe as 'drugs of last resort'. These are compounds like vancomycin and methicillin, which are the only ones left that kill some antibiotic resistant mutants of common infections. When bacteria mutate to become resistant to these antibiotics doctors will have no weapons left to protect us from the infections.

Antibiotic resistance is one of the most pressing problems in medicine. In the United States, antibiotic resistant infections that people catch during their stay in hospital lead to an estimated 60,000 deaths per year.

The nightmare scenario, of a lethal bacterium that's resistant to all known antibiotics, might not be far away. Then we might see a return to the kind of plagues that killed millions in the Middle Ages.

Many scientists are understandably worried about using antibiotic resistance as reporter genes in genetically-engineered organisms. We don't want more antibiotic resistance introduced into the environment, encouraging the evolution of still more resistant bacteria.

That's why, in December 1996, the British government tried to block imports of an American genetically-engineered maize variety. It contains a reporter gene for antibiotic resistance, which allowed the genetic engineers to identify their novel plant while it was just a few cells in a dish in the laboratory. There are fears that this resistance gene would be transmitted from the plant cells to bacteria in the guts of cattle that ate the maize. These bacteria might then pass their genes to bacteria that live in human guts, with awful consequences.

Situations like this highlight another problem that rears its ugly head when governments try to control the use of genetic engineering. These modified organisms don't need passports – they can slip backwards and forwards across national borders unnoticed.

No frontiers

➤Imagine this situation.

You live in a country where genetic engineering experiments are tightly controlled, so that unpleasant accidents are unlikely. It all seems pretty safe. But scientists in a neighbouring country are not restricted in the same way. Their government urgently wants them to develop new kinds of transgenic viruses that will kill pests.

They spray their genetically-engineered viruses on fields. Then the inevitable happens. The viruses cross the border, carried by wind, water or maybe even on car tyres, and spread. Worse still, instead of just killing pests, they begin to wipe out harmless butterflies and beneficial insects.

There's nothing you can do about it. Your government can protest, but the accident has already happened. The deadly virus is on the rampage.

In 1994 European and American companies were still carrying out cautious experiments with genetically-engineered organisms. So, many western scientists were shocked to discover that China had already planted thousands of hectares of genetically-engineered crops, without the same safety checks.

Today, governments are still trying to agree on international rules for genetic engineering and the release of genetically-engineered organisms. At the moment every country makes its own rules. In some they're extremely strict. In others there are none at all.

In 1995, in an effort to test existing regulations on transport of genetically-engineered organisms, Greenpeace International posted 18 packages to nine different countries around the world. Each carried clear labels declaring that they contained genetically modified organisms or biological materials. The US, Russian and Swiss postal services delivered packages labelled as 'genetically modified materials' to private addresses, which could easily have been the homes of terrorists. Three packages were leaking when they arrived. Two disappeared completely in the post. If any of these had contained real, genetically-engineered microbes that were dangerous to humans, the consequences might have been horrendous.

In 1991 three laboratories in Britain were caught carrying out illegal genetic experiments on micro-organisms.

There's nothing to stop scientists in some countries from developing genetic engineering programmes on deadly organisms that could be used in germ warfare, to create ecological havoc or to infect people. There's nothing to stop them developing new strains of bacteria or viruses in any way they please.

Genetically-engineered organisms don't recognize political boundaries when they're released into the environment. If we don't have regulations that govern every country on Earth, why bother to have any regulations at all?

Genetically-engineered plants, animals, bacteria and viruses can move long distances, as the accident with calicivirus in Australia has shown. The safety of genetic engineering worldwide depends on what happens in countries with the weakest regulations. And when some countries have no regulations at all, anything could happen.

In 1986, when safety regulations in the United States became too tough and time-consuming for testing a new rabies vaccine, one group of American University scientists moved their genetic engineering experiments to Argentina. Since then at least one European genetic engineering company has threatened to dodge difficult safety regulations at home by moving to a country where there are fewer restrictions on its work.

A survey by Greenpeace International in 1994 revealed that illegal releases of genetically-engineered organisms have taken place in Argentina, Kenya, India and Ireland.

Hope

➤There is a tailpiece to the myth of Pandora's box, which is usually forgotten.

Hope, one of the Three Graces of Greek legend, remained at the bottom of Pandora's box when the fateful lid was lifted. She alone has the power to ease man's troubles and sorrows.

And there is hope that scientists can solve problems by using genetically-engineered micro-organisms. There is hope that antibiotic-resistant bacteria can be defeated.

Even now researchers are experimenting with new compounds called peptides – small fragments of proteins – that protect some animals from bacterial diseases. One of these chemicals is called magainin, a name which comes from the Hebrew word for a shield. It's found in the skin of frogs. These compounds work in a different way to antibiotics and so far bacteria haven't been able to develop resistance to them. Compounds like magainin could provide a new defence against antibiotic-resistant bacteria.

Section Thirteen

GREEN GENES

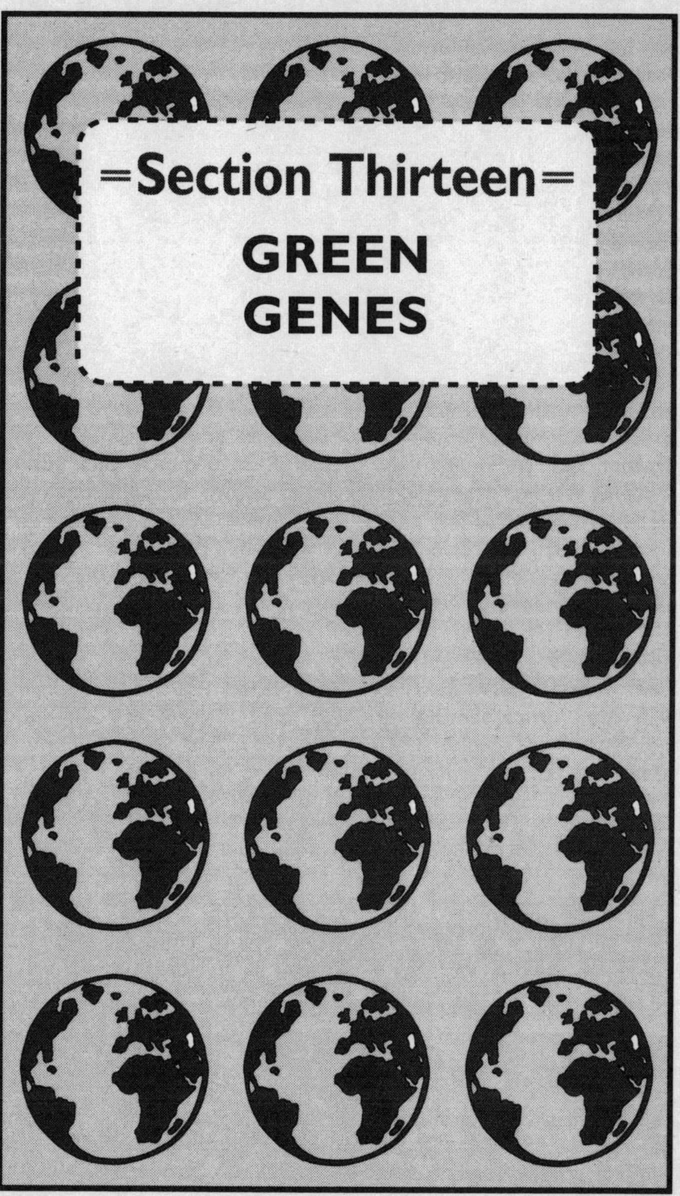

As our numbers increase, we humans are rapidly using up Earth's natural resources. At the same time we're creating pollution that's contaminating the air, seas and soil. And when we burn fossil fuel like coal, gas and oil we are changing the composition of the atmosphere and altering the climate around the world.

Finding environmentally-friendly ways to live without destroying our planet has never been more important.

The heat is on

➤Global climate change could turn out to be the most disastrous effect that we humans have had on our environment.

By burning fossil fuels like gas, oil and coal, we have pumped ever-greater levels of carbon dioxide into the atmosphere. This has increased the power of the greenhouse effect, where gases like carbon dioxide trap heat from sunlight, stopping it from escaping back into space. So, as the carbon dioxide level rises, the atmosphere is getting warmer and the weather is changing. Most scientists agree that global warming is under way.

Climatologists say that this could turn some areas where we grow food into deserts. It could melt the ice caps and glaciers, so that rising sea levels flood low-lying countries. It could create violent storms.

It's too late to stop the first effects of global warming – glaciers in the Alps are already melting, the sea level is already rising and there have been several droughts that have damaged crop production in various parts of the world. But we could stop it getting worse, if we could find a substitute for fossil fuels and cut down the amount of carbon dioxide that we generate.

Pollution-free fuel

➤Hydrogen is a promising pollution-free fuel. When it burns, it combines with oxygen and releases energy. The only waste product is water vapour, which eventually falls back to earth as precious rain.

There's one major drawback: hydrogen is very costly to produce. It's made by splitting water molecules, which releases hydrogen and oxygen, but this process needs a lot of expensive energy. But now genetic engineers may have found a cheap, environmentally-friendly way to produce hydrogen, so that it could eventually provide the fuel for our cars and power stations.

They've managed it by developing genetically-engineered bacteria that release enzymes that can convert glucose in plants into pollution-free hydrogen fuel.

The process is still in its infancy, but the beauty of this piece of genetic trickery is that it could produce hydrogen fuel in a way that recycles carbon dioxide in the atmosphere without making the problem of global warming worse. Plants use carbon dioxide from the atmosphere to make glucose; we use the glucose to make hydrogen. Even the waste product from the process – gluconic acid – is valuable; it's used in all sorts of industrial chemical processes.

Paper power

➤One day we will probably be growing crops that genetically-engineered bacteria will turn into hydrogen fuel, but we could also use the same process to turn waste paper into hydrogen.

Paper is made from cellulose, the raw material that plants are constructed from. Cellulose can be converted into glucose. Then the bacterial enzymes could take over and turn that into hydrogen.

It's been calculated that the United States produces enough waste newspaper every year to provide hydrogen fuel for 37 small cities, if it could all be converted into hydrogen.

Hydrogen hazards

➤Any problems? Probably. No new technology is ever risk-free.

Hydrogen is a dangerously explosive fuel that needs careful handling. Cars, power stations and domestic heating systems would have to be modified before they could use it. There may be other steps in its production that can generate pollutants. And if it was used as an aircraft fuel it would still create problems because water vapour trapped in the stratosphere, where airliners fly, acts as a greenhouse gas.

But it's likely that most of these problems can be overcome. In the long term, enzymes from genetically-engineered bacteria could play a key role in reducing planetary pollution.

Meal menance

➤Two centuries of heavy industry have left us with a legacy of polluted land that's a danger to human health. Cancer-causing wastes from the chemical industry and toxic heavy metals like lead, cadmium and zinc make some land too dangerous to disturb. But now genetic engineers may have found a solution.

Plants have been found with genes that make them immune to high levels of heavy metals that would kill normal plants. The next step is to transfer these to crops that would act as pollution scavengers, soaking up the poisonous compounds from contaminated land. It might even be possible to extract the metal from the plants and recycle it.

Bacteria have been developed which can also accumulate or break down pollutants. One species has been found that 'eats' pesticides and makes them harmless. It might be just the thing for removing dangerous pesticides from contaminated water.

But, as always, there are questions that need to be answered before any of these laboratory-bred life forms are let loose in the environment:

☐ Can pollution-accumulating bacteria swap genetic information with others in the environment, and so spread into places where they might be a menace?

☐ Can pollen from pollution-accumulating crops reach nearby weeds and produce hybrids that will escape into the wild? This would produce populations of wild plants that might look normal, but which could build up dangerous levels of poisons.

☐ If insects feed on plants that are loaded with pollutants, will they then be eaten by mammals, concentrating the poisons at every step? What started out as a small amount of a heavy metal in a pollution-busting plant could be passed along the food chain, in ever-higher concentrations, and end up as a fatal dose in a bird. This kind of thing has happened before, when the insecticide

DDT finally accumulated in birds, threatening the survival of some species.

□ Can we be sure that heavy metal-accumulating genes won't be transferred through pollen to food crops, so that the toxins enter the human food chain?

Before breakthroughs in genetic engineering can be turned into practical solutions, these kinds of risks need to be investigated thoroughly. We need to be sure that we won't repeat past mistakes, or make new ones that could be even worse. Genes from a jellyfish may help.

Bright idea

Genespeak
Bioluminescence – the way in which many sea creatures and some insects and fungi emit light in the darkness.

➤Many sea creatures contain bioluminescent substances that make them glow with eerie green and blue lights. One such animal is the jellyfish Aequorea victorea, which contains a beautiful green protein that makes it glow. Colourful chemical compounds like these could provide the key to following the fate of dangerous genes in the environment.

If genes for the green fluorescent protein from Aequorea are inserted into plants, they'll be transferred from plant to plant in the pollen. If the genes are spreading, green fluorescent plants will turn up everywhere. If they're not, plants like this will be rare.

By striding through fields after dark, shining ultra-violet spotlights on plants, ecologists will be able to find the glowing, genetically-engineered plants that have escaped. The same jellyfish gene can be inserted into bacteria, plants, animals and fungi, to follow their genes around. It's genetic engineering's brightest idea yet for monitoring the risks from the new organisms.

Regreening the land

➤In some parts of the world there are soils that are so heavily contaminated with herbicides that no plants will grow on them. In Canada a variety of flax plant, called Triffid, has had to be developed that is immune to herbicide residues that remain in the soil after wheat crops have been grown.

This strategy, where plants are genetically engineered to tolerate polluted soils, is another possible way of reclaiming land that has been lost through misuse in the past.

One of the world's worst agricultural problems is the build-up of salt in soil. It happens when crops are irrigated with water pumped from deep wells. The water evaporates from the soil surface, leaving a crust of toxic salt crystals.

It's a problem that has been with us for thousands of years. Archaeologists have discovered that crop production in ancient Mesopotamia in 1700 BC declined dramatically because the ancient farmers over-irrigated their land, which became too salty for wheat cultivation.

The Chinese have lived with the problem for years. There, some farmers remove salt from their land by growing plants that naturally thrive on coastal salt marshes.

These species accumulate salt from the soil and store it as harmless crystals in their leaves. When the crop is harvested, the salt is removed. After a few cycles of growing plants like this, the soil salt level drops and normal food crops can be grown again.

Now biologists are beginning to discover bacterial genes that protect plants from high salt levels. They're transferring these to crop plants, which will then grow on salty soils that would destroy most crops. In this way, land that has been lost to cultivation can be restored to food production.

One possible hazard from breeding these salt tolerant crops is that they might invade natural coastal habitats that are wildlife refuges. They would also make it possible for people to cultivate these wild habitats, posing further threats to dwindling species of wild plants and animals that live there.

With every application of genetic engineering technology, it's important to try to foresee problems that could turn a useful breakthrough into an ecological catastrophe.

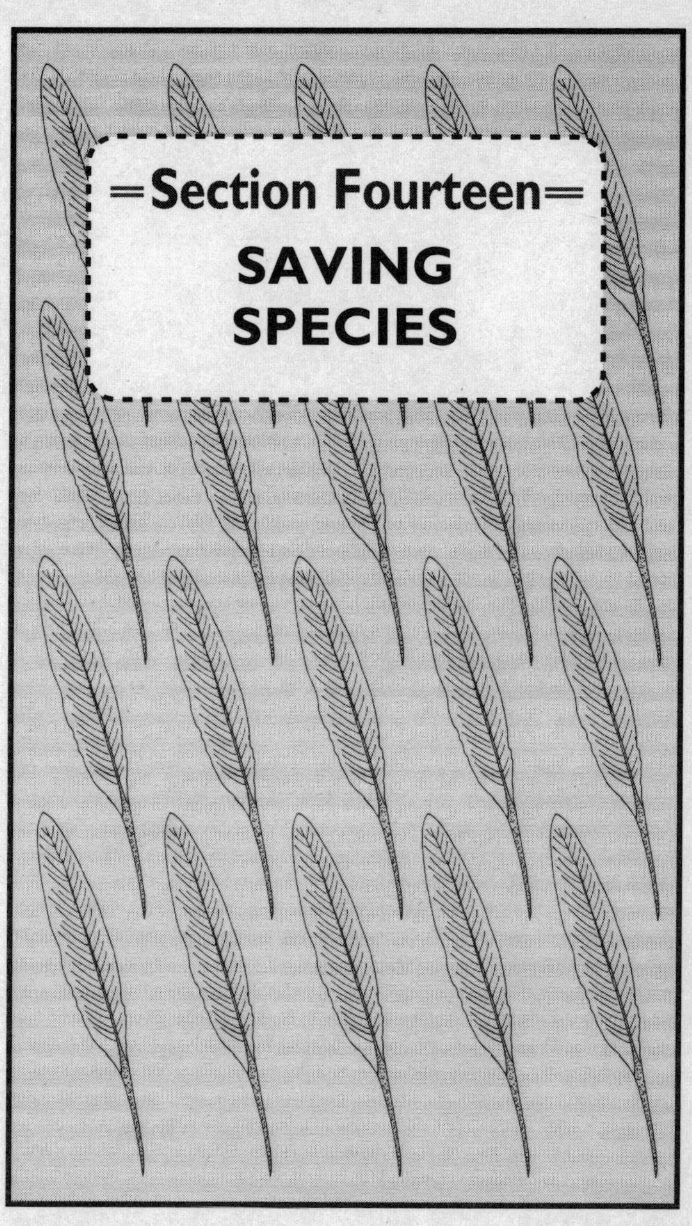
Section Fourteen
SAVING
SPECIES

Who's a pretty boy, then?

➤Countless parrot owners have taught their pets to say 'Who's a pretty boy, then?', only to discover that the parrot has laid an egg and must be a pretty girl after all.

The plumage of male and female parrots is often so similar that it's impossible to tell them apart. Fortunately, geneticists can help. By extracting DNA from just one feather, they can identify the sex of a parrot.

This kind of information is extremely important for zoos that are trying to pair up males and females of rare parrot species in breeding programmes, in attempts to increase their dwindling numbers. It may even help to save the critically endangered Spix macaw from extinction.

Until recently there was only one very lonely Spix macaw left in the wild. Other captive birds exist in collections and conservationists have been keen to release one so that it could pair with the last wild survivor. With luck they might mate and start a new wild breeding population. But until they knew the sex of the last wild macaw, there was no point in releasing a captive bird. They could have ended up with two males or two females in the wild, with no hope of any eggs.

Fortunately the wild macaw moulted a feather. Geneticists were able to extract a minute amount of DNA from it and show that it was from a male bird. A suitable mate has been released. Now conservationists wait with bated breath to see if the two birds pair and reproduce.

The case of the lonely Spix macaw is just one of a growing number of uses of DNA in conserving wildlife. It's a technology that has brought new hope to the fight to protect endangered species.

Protecting peregrines

➤Birds of prey are declining in many parts of the world. Sometimes they are wiped out by persecution, loss of habitat and poisoning by pesticides. But there's also a thriving international trade in illegally captured birds. People like to own these exotic animals, and will pay a high price for eggs and chicks.

In many countries governments have brought in laws to protect dwindling species like peregrine falcons. In Britain, for example, it is illegal to take young peregrines from their nests and keep them in captivity. But laws like this aren't always easy to enforce. Unscrupulous people still rob nests, taking eggs and young birds that they sell to falconers abroad.

Until recently, thieves could escape prosecution when they were caught with captive peregrines. They could claim that the birds were raised from eggs that had been laid by captive peregrines, that had been caught legally before the new, stricter laws were introduced.

But DNA technology has closed this loophole in the law. Now DNA fingerprints can be taken from all peregrines that are legally held in captivity, and the suspect birds' DNA can be compared with them. If the DNA samples don't show the matching patterns that you would expect between parents and chicks, you can be sure that the chicks must have been taken from nests in the wild.

DNA fingerprinting of birds of prey has already convicted several egg thieves.

DNA can reveal the identity of a species from a small sample of its flesh. Tests on DNA in whale steaks sold in Japanese restaurants have shown that illegal whaling, that threatens rare whale species, still goes on.

Back from the brink

➤The numbers of individuals in many rare plant and animal species has declined drastically. When this happens the species can become extinct very quickly. Conservationists often need to make last-ditch attempts to rebuild the populations by breeding the rare species in captivity, but this process can be tricky.

Healthy wild populations of plants and animals have plenty of genetic variation. Every individual is slightly different genetically from its neighbour. This variation between individuals is a kind of natural insurance policy for the species. If conditions change, this reservoir of potentially useful genes means that there will always be some individuals that are adapted to thrive in new surroundings.

But, as populations shrink, the survivors only carry a small amount of the genetic variation that once existed in the whole species. And once their numbers fall to a critical level, the pool of genetic variation shrinks even more, as closely related individuals breed with one another. This kind of inbreeding often causes infertility and birth defects.

So conservationists always try to cross-breed individuals from a species that are as different as possible from one another. This maintains a high, healthy level of genetic variation in the population. But how can you tell whether two animals are closely related? Genetic engineering technology comes to the rescue again.

Scientists can take a DNA sample from a hair of a mammal or a feather of a bird and compare it with others in the population. Then they can choose pairs for breeding that are as different as possible from one another. In time, by a careful choice of parents, they can rebuild populations with enough genetic variability to survive the trials and tribulations of a changing environment in the wild.

For some time, biologists have suspected that pipistrelle bats with slightly different squeaks might be a separate species. Recently DNA tests have proved they're right. We now know that Britain has two species of pipistrelle, not one, thanks to DNA testing.

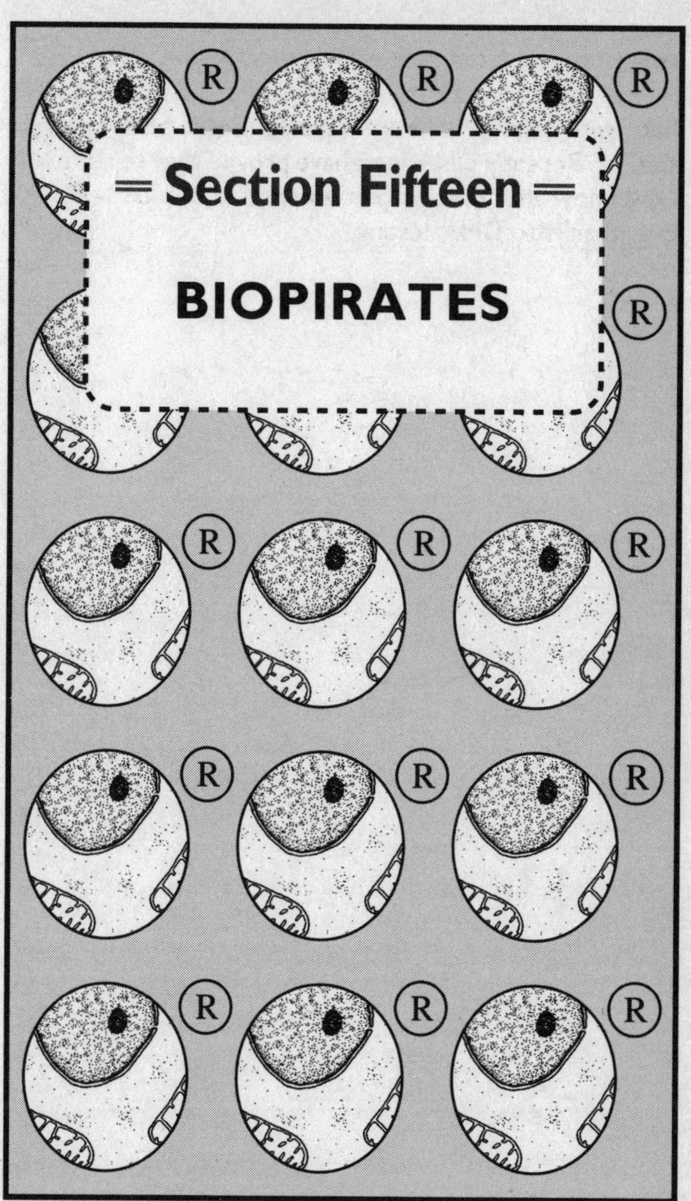
Section Fifteen
BIOPIRATES
R

In December 1994, after two years of surveillance, FBI agents swooped on two employees of an American biotechnology company. One of the arrested men was thought to have links with the old Soviet secret service, the KGB. The secret agents suspected that the men were stealing genetically-engineered cells. The cells contained a gene that made a drug called erythropoietin, which helps AIDS and cancer patients to produce red blood cells.

The FBI agents claimed that the two employees planned to sell the stolen cells to a foreign company for $300,000. This would have been the bargain of the century. It would have cost $100 million in research and development costs to genetically engineer the cells from scratch. With the stolen cells it would cost the company less than $1 million.

Genes are big business. The world market for the erythropoietin made by the stolen cells is worth about $1 billion. So it's hardly surprising that companies are desperate to get into the genetic engineering business. There are vast fortunes to be made. The whole industry has been compared with the California gold rush of the 19th century.

Patent protection

> *'The purpose of patents is to promote "the Progress of Science and the Useful Arts, by securing for limited times to authors and inventors the exclusive right to their respective writings and discoveries . . ." '*
> *(Extract from the United States Constitution)*

➤Before genetically-engineered organisms can make money, they must become someone's legal property, so that they can't be copied and sold by everyone.

At least, that's what the biotechnology industry claims. And they have a point. Would you want to spend vast amounts of time and money creating a new invention if someone else could copy and sell it, without paying you a penny?

Inventions are legally protected by patents. These are documents that give the inventor sole rights to make and sell the invention. If anyone else wants to make the same product, they have to obtain a licence from the inventor and pay them royalties (a proportion of their profits) on every copy of the invention they make. Anyone who makes the invention without a licence can be prosecuted in court.

So patents on inventions serve several purposes:

- ☐ They encourage companies to invest money in new inventions.
- ☐ They help to ensure that they profit from them.
- ☐ They prevent other people from stealing inventions and selling them as their own.

They also create some strange legal conflicts. Today, a farmer whose cow has a calf owns the cow and the calf. In the future, if a cow has a calf that's sired by a genetically-engineered bull whose genes have been patented by a genetic engineering company, then the calf will belong to the company that owns the gene patent, not the farmer.

And if farmers save seeds from a genetically-engineered crop, to plant again next year, they'll be infringing the seed company's patent and breaking the law. It will be no different in law from making an illegal 'bootleg' copy of a music tape or video.

Patenting living organisms will change the way we view the natural world.

Secret science

➤You can only patent an invention if no one else knows about it already. Secrecy during product development is vital. This means that much of the genetic engineering that's going on is done out of sight, in secret. We can't ask questions or object about what's going on, because there's no way of finding out about it until the work has been completed and patented.

There was a time when it was usual for scientists to collaborate on projects and share information about their breakthroughs. This meant that they didn't waste time and money duplicating each other's work. Not any more. Now profits from patents are so important that they often work in secret, so that they can beat their rivals to money-spinning discoveries. This kind of secrecy can slow down research in important areas, like the search for cancer cures.

Can you really patent life?

➤The battle lines have been drawn up between people who find the patenting of genes repugnant and the genetic engineering executives who say it's vital for the future of the industry. Stand between them and you'd hear arguments like this flying back and forth:

- No one should be allowed to own genes. They're the basic building blocks of life and they should be the property of the human race, not multinational corporations.
- If we put huge amounts of money into developing useful genetically-engineered products, then we deserve to get

the maximum reward.

- Patents were designed to protect new inventions. How can you call a gene a new invention? They were there all the time. They were discovered, not invented.
- If you won't let us patent genes, it won't be worth investing money in the industry, so mankind won't reap any of the benefits.
- If you patent genes, it means that the poor countries that need genetically-engineered crops and medicines most won't be able to use them, unless they pay you for licences that they can't afford.
- Poor countries can't afford to develop this kind of advanced technology on their own. They rely on our scientists, but we can't provide their services for nothing. The royalties from patents are a small price to pay for our help.
- If you own patents on genes, you can stop other people working with them. If they have good ideas but can't afford the royalties you demand, you are stopping progress.

'Greedy patenting could starve the poor of biotech promise.'
(Headline, *New Scientist*, 16 November 1996)

'. . . biotechnology patents held by companies will create a "scientific apartheid", which locks the 80 per cent of people in developing countries out of scientific advances.'
(Opinion of Ismail Serageldin, speaking at the UN World Food Summit, November 1996, quoted in* New Scientist*)

Gene prospecting

➤Genetic engineering seems set to make enormous sums of money for biotechnology companies, but their success depends on a ready supply of raw materials – genes. So gene prospectors are scouring the world for useful genes.

Some are searching in tropical rainforests for plant genes that make valuable medicines. Finding these would be almost impossible without help from local people, who have used the forest plants as medicines for years. They can tell the gene prospectors where to look. No one seems sure whether the local communities will get a financial reward for providing the knowledge that scientists need to find these natural resources.

Other teams of scientists are looking for genes in people. One American company is already trying to patent thousands of human genes, even though they don't know what the genes do. Some of them may be vital for the development of multimillion-dollar cures for major diseases.

Still more companies are concentrating on genes in bacteria, especially if these come from extreme environments like hot water around undersea volcanoes, or the frozen wastes of the Arctic. Bacteria that live at low temperatures, for example, contain strange fats which stay soft at low temperatures and may have industrial uses.

Gene prospectors are scouring the world for potential products. But not everyone is happy. Some say that they're not prospectors, they're thieves.

Gene theft

➤For most of this century, scientists from plant-breeding companies have been searching Third World countries for genes that can be used to protect plants from disease.

These have then been taken back to Europe and North America and used to breed new, improved crops which generate profits for the companies concerned.

Until recently the Third World countries, who were the source of the money-spinning genes in the first place, have got very little from the deal. In most cases they have had to pay to use genes originally discovered in their own countries, when they have had to pay high prices to use the improved crops.

As far as plant genes are concerned, you can divide the world into two halves.

The technologically advanced, financially wealthy, industrialized regions, like Europe and North America, are gene poor.

Almost all the major crops that they grow originally came from the other half of the world – the gene rich, financially poor Third World.

So when plant breeding companies need more genes to improve crops, they head south, out into the remote regions of poor countries in Africa, India or South America.

But Third World countries have had enough of this exploitation. They're tired of watching rich nations plunder their natural genetic resources, for no benefit to their impoverished citizens. And so countries like India have now introduced 'gene theft' laws making it illegal to take genes or living organisms out of their country without a permit.

In the old days scientific expeditions set off into the interior of tropical countries and came back laden with crates of plants or animals that they shipped home. Those days are gone. Today they would find themselves in jail, unless they had already signed legally binding agreements that would ensure that some of their profits would find their way back to the source of the living organisms that they'd collected.

Fair shares for all

➤Legal arguments are still raging in several countries over who should share in the profits made from valuable gene discoveries, but some people are benefiting already.

In India a drug called jeevani, that combats stress and provides an instant source of energy, has been extracted for centuries from a native plant called Trichopus zeylnicus. The plant's value was first discovered by members of the Kani tribe, who live in the Agasthiyar Hills in Kerala State. Now foreign pharmaceutical companies want to manufacture the drug for worldwide sale, so the Indian government has negotiated a deal. Kani farmers who cultivate the plant own the patent and will receive two per cent of the profits on worldwide sales.

Deals are also likely to be struck with individual people whose bodies provide DNA samples that lead to useful gene discoveries, although no one has come up with any totally acceptable ways for doing this. One possibility, proposed in the United States, is that people who give up the rights to useful genes that they might have should be rewarded with free healthcare for life, while a percentage of profits from any useful products would go to humanitarian charities.

But in some parts of the world the whole idea of patenting human genes has raised a whirlwind of controversy.

The 'vampire' project

'Over the last 200 years, non-Aboriginal people have taken our lands, language, culture, health – even our children. Now they want to take the genetic material that makes us Aboriginal people as well.'
(John Liddle, Director, Central Australian Aboriginal Congress, 1994)

Genespeak
Genome – the complete set of genes possessed by an organism.
Anthropologist – a scientist who studies human evolution.
Human Genome Diversity Project – a project designed to collect information about the genetic variation in the human race.

➤The Human Genome Diversity Project has been designed to allow scientists and anthropologists to find out more about the origins of the human race. By taking small blood samples from people, researchers can compare their DNA and learn all kinds of fascinating information. Information from the patterns of distribution of genes in different places can tell us much about human evolution. It can build up a picture of the ways in which different nations and tribes have migrated across the surface of our planet.

It can also tell us how different groups of people have evolved to resist disease. That information has turned out to be political dynamite, as scientists who are studying tribes in New Guinea have found to their cost.

The Hagahai are a small tribe that live in the remote hills of Papua New Guinea. There are only 293 people in the tribe, who had never been seen by visitors from the outside world until 1984.

Recently scientists arrived in Papua to take blood samples from them, as part of the Human Genome Diversity Project. To their amazement, the scientists discovered that some of these people carried a gene that made them immune to a deadly virus that caused a form of cancer when it infected other people.

The scientists took a few Hagahai cells infected with the virus back to the United States, grew them in the laboratory and then patented the cells. So now the genetic properties of a citizen of a poor foreign country were legally owned by the United States government. The Hagahai tribesman whose body supplied the cells didn't own his own genetic material any more, but it was obvious that these cells and the genes they contained could be a massive moneyspinner if they could be used to help develop a cure for the cancer virus.

It has to be said that this was done with the permission of the tribe member who produced the cells, and that the Hagahai would probably gain a share of any commercial profits from the discovery. But when they learned what had happened, most of the indigenous peoples of the world believed that it was an outrage. Alejandro Argumedo, of the Indigenous People's Biodiversity Network, described it as 'the most offensive patent ever issued.'

Accusations flew. Tempers flared.

Eventually, at the end of 1996, the United States National Institute of Health finally dropped its controversial claim on the Hagahai cells – because the likely profits from using the cells wouldn't have been as great as they had hoped.

But the damage had been done. A project that had started off as innocent science revealed how much the Third World distrusted the developed world's intentions, and exchanges like this became a familiar feature of scientific conferences:

Third World Scientist: How can native tribesmen, who can't read or write, really understand what was being done with their DNA? This is just like the old days, when western explorers exchanged beads and trinkets for gold nuggets, exploiting the innocence of tribesmen to get their hands on their valuable resources. Collecting useful human genes from our citizens is the worst case yet of the rich nations exploiting the resources of the poor.

Western Scientist: We're not stealing your resources! When we collect genes, we do it because they can be used for medical treatments that will benefit mankind. We can't afford to do this for nothing, so we've taken out a patent. That means we'll make money from the products that we develop, which will help pay for our costs. And eventually we'll be giving some of the money to the tribesmen.

Third World Scientist: You're not being completely honest. If these genes are so valuable, and can provide products that can be used in medicine throughout the world, then you'll make vast sums of money. Only a minute fraction of that will come back to the countries whose people provided the genes in the first place. In fact, they'll probably find themselves having to pay for the medicines you develop with the help of their genes.

Some of our small tribes are now threatened with extinction, either because their land has been stolen or because they have caught diseases from foreigners. It seems to us that the Human Genome Diversity Project is more interested in collecting genes than helping our people. It looks suspiciously like the project was designed to collect poor people's genes before it's too late, and use them to make medical companies in wealthy nations even wealthier.

Genespeak
Indigenous people – the people who first settled in different places on Earth.

All over the planet, the indigenous peoples of the world, ranging from Australian Aborigines to North American Indians, have sworn that they'll have nothing to do with the project. They produced a declaration designed to fend off what they saw as predatory western scientists.

To the indigenous peoples of the world, the Human Genome Diversity Project has become known as the 'Vampire Project', designed to sample their blood and steal their genes. And they call the western governments and scientists involved 'biopirates'.

'We oppose the patenting of all natural genetic materials. We hold that life cannot be bought, owned, sold, discovered or patented, even in its smallest form.'
(Extract from the Declaration of Indigenous Peoples of the Western Hemisphere, 19 February 1995, Phoenix, Arizona)

Everything has its price

➤It does seem that the Third World might eventually profit from the great gene goldrush. Breakthroughs in studies of the genes will eventually generate wealth and some of it will trickle down to the poorer nations, provided that international law supports their fight to retain ownership of their own genetic resources.

But many people the world over now view the way the natural world is being exploited by the biotechnology industry with a tinge of sadness. They see a time coming when the value of every living organism might depend on how much money its genes are worth.

Everything in the living world will carry a price tag.

Genespeak
Technocrat – a person who has complete, unquestioning confidence in the beneficial power of technology.

'The technocrat does not question the human right to control nature . . . The technocrat looks forward to the day when humans will have complete control over the earth.'
(Alan R. Dregson, Canadian philosopher)

Section Sixteen
WHAT WOULD YOU DO?
R

Gregor Mendel, the Abbot of Brünn who discovered the laws of genetics, could never have guessed that the science he created would become such a powerful force for changing the world.

In future almost every aspect of our lives will be affected in some way by the science of genetics and by the technology of genetic engineering. Medicine, food production, industrial products, the environment, law and order, politics and international trade – and even our choice of partners for personal relationships – could be affected in some way.

Is it something we should welcome, or is there serious cause for concern?

One important thing to remember is that the technology itself is just a set of techniques that can be used for a wide variety of purposes. The genetic engineering process was designed to allow scientists to swap genes around between distantly related organisms, like plants and animals. Some people might oppose that use because they see it as unnatural interference in nature. But many of the processes that have arisen from the same technology – such as genetic fingerprinting – are also extremely valuable for applications that most people would approve of, such as wildlife conservation or catching criminals.

Some applications of genetics will be good, some not so good and some downright bad. Just like any other technology, it's the way that it's used that's really important, not the technology itself.

Electricity, for example, can be used as a power source for life-saving medical equipment in a hospital, or as a power source for electric chairs for executing criminals in America, or as a power source for equipment used to torture political prisoners in some other parts of the world. It's applications that are the really important issues, not the basic scientific principles that make them possible.

You may have noticed a common thread running through many applications of genetic engineering: its potential for generating huge profits for companies involved. One symptom of this can be found in some of the products that have appeared so far – long-life tomatoes, blue roses and potatoes that make better crisps – all money-spinning, trivial consumer products that don't have much direct impact on the plight of starving people in developing countries. Somehow we need to ensure – perhaps through international agencies – that the technology really does help the people who need it most.

The race for profits also means that there are many ways in which genetic engineering could be abused or could cause serious accidents that would do permanent environmental damage. National governments, dazzled by the prospect of a new industry that could generate great wealth, may be tempted to relax safety testing regulations. But safety in the industry is an international issue. Genetically engineered micro-organisms don't recognize national boundaries, and there's an urgent need for a worldwide organization with the authority to dictate the ground rules for the technology.

Their problem would be to decide how and when we should use genetic engineering, and to try to avoid making bad decisions that might cause human suffering and environmental damage. They would have to examine each individual application and rely on the four principles that are laid down by the science of ethics. For each application they'd need to ask:

Does it restrict freedom – of people and, perhaps, also of animals?

Eugenics, for example, quite obviously restricted people's freedom to have children if they were believed to carry 'bad' genes. So this application of the technology is obviously wrong.

Does it go against natural justice?

You might argue, for example, that it would be extremely unfair if European or North American drugs companies patented genes for useful drugs taken from medicinal plants that are used by Amazonian indigenous tribes. They discovered the uses of the plants, showed scientists where to find them and how to use them, and at the very least deserve a generous share of future profits that the drugs might generate.

Is it harmless?

This is a question that can be applied to almost any genetically-engineered organism that will be released into the environment. It's this question that creates the need for extensive safety testing and international regulations to control the release of genetically-engineered organisms.

Is it unkind?

This is the question that we must ask for any genetic engineering process carried out on animals and people. If the genetic changes create suffering, then they fail this test.

You might like to try these questions yourself, on some of the applications that have been described in this book. Test them out on the following questions, and see what you think:

☐ Do the benefits of genetic testing of humans outweigh the risks?

☐ Should companies be allowed to patent living organisms?

☐ Should herbicide resistant crops be grown?

☐ Should scientists be allowed to alter the characteristics of people before birth, by altering the eggs or sperm that form embryos?

☐ Should we breed genetically-engineered farm animals that produce drugs instead of food?

☐ Should everyone's DNA fingerprint be on a police database?

☐ Would you like to see all genetically-engineered foods labelled?

☐ Would you buy a tropical food product that had been made by cells under laboratory conditions in a factory, rather than in a plant in a farmers field?

Examining every aspect of questions like these can help us to form opinions that can be the basis for democratic decisions about the new technology. But it's not quite as easy as it seems.

Think back to the imaginary situation at the beginning of the book, where your loved one is lying in hospital, waiting for a heart transplant from a pig. It fails most – maybe even all – of the ethical tests because it conflicts with concerns for animal welfare and animal rights, and because it hasn't been proved that it will be harmless. We still don't know whether pig organs carry unknown diseases.

When it comes to making decisions about whether actions are morally right or wrong, our personal situation plays a major role in our conclusions.

If your life – or the life of a loved one – depended on a heart transplant from a pig, would you refuse?